Angling Guide to Colorado's Blue Mesa Reservoir

By Andy Lightbody

127 Hottest Fishing Spots

The Best Angling Advice

Global Positioning Systems Coordinates

96 Places for the Best Food, Lodging and
Recreation in Gunnison Country

North Cape Publications

This book is dedicated to all my family—unique outdoor folks, one and all:

Ray "I'll drive the boat" Lightbody
Betty "You all smell so fishy" Lightbody
Daniel "How come they aren't biting" Lightbody
Jeffrey "Splash" Lightbody
Matthew "NO" Lightbody
Jennifer "Fishies" Lightbody
And my wife, Tari—who I fell for hook, line and sinker—not so long ago.

This publication is designed to provide authoritative and accurate information in regard to the subject matter covered. However, it should be recognized that information provided herein is based on the author's own experience and that of others and is necessarily limited by access to what are largely remote areas. Every effort has been made to assure all coordinates and directions are correct.

ISBN 1-882391-10-1
North Cape Publications, P.O. Box 1027, Tustin, California 92681
714 832-3621

Printed in USA by Complete Reproduction Services, Santa Ana, California, USA

Table of Contents

Forward

No book that really is a "first in it's field" has one single author. While I've spent the last several years compiling information about all of the great fishing and camping spots that can he found on the Blue Mesa Reservoir, my research is, in fact, the result of many people's contributions and their generous willingness to share information.

As the saying goes, an expert is someone "who knows where to go and who to ask for the answers." Without great contacts, this book could not have been written. After all, when you boldly go where no writer has gone before, you can't be every place at the right time. But with so many people helping and encouraging me to compile the data on fishing locations and hot-spots on Colorado's largest lake, I hope that you will be as pleased with this "first" book on summer fishing on the Blue Mesa Reservoir, as I am. And I hope that subsequent editions of this book, as well as additional writings by other authors and magazine writers will add more hot-spots, fishing techniques and angling secrets for this unique body of water.

I want to thank the following individuals and businesses for their generous and unstinting help and support in the preparation of this Guide: The Loken family and employees of the Elk Creek and Lake Fork Marinas, as well as the Blue Mesa Ranch, for boats whenever needed, for hot tips, great guiding and continuing trust; Pappy's Restaurant for wonderful early morning breakfasts and super lunches; Steve and Keith Fry and Mary Kay Penning of Gunnison Sporting Goods for help in taking me to many of their "hot-spots" and letting me write about them; Phil Zickerman, Chief of Interpretation for the U.S. National Park Service at the Gunnison River Territory's Curecanti Recreation Area on the Blue Mesa Reservoir; Jim Young, District Manager for Colorado Division of Wildlife (DoW) in Gunnison; Scott Petersen for always being there for so many early morning fishing trips; The Lazy-K Resort for hosting lots of Outdoor Writers/Editors that in turn added to my personal angling knowledge; the Pike family—Jim, Steve, Paul and Bobbie—for showing me how to find and catch those "feisty" brook trout; and the fine folks at Gene Taylor's Sporting Goods—Don Mills, Sr., Don Mills, Jr. and Pat Strahl.

A special thanks also to one of the premiere fishing families of the Gunnison area—the Reillys. Matt, Pat, Marilyn and Chris have my many thanks for all the fishing trips they, and especially Matt, organized that helped me explore the Gunnison River Territory from one end to another. In day's gone by, you folks made researching and writing this Guide a lot of fun and extremely informative.

Finally a big and most grateful thank you to my family for allowing me the time, space and opportunity to compile all this "expert" information. My wife, Tari—also an author—was extremely helpful in compiling and my often turgid prose. And to my folks, Ray and Betty Lightbody for teaching me at an early age to love the outdoors and to share my experiences with others. A special thanks to my Dad and my sons, Daniel and Jeffrey, for their help and assistance in the GPS mapping process of the Blue Mesa Reservoir. It took us nearly a year and a half to map all the Global Positioning Satellite (GPS) locations included in the following pages. But now that we have them listed, they are yours.

After extensive use of the Global Positioning System, I know that anyone, from 8 years old to 80, can use the GPS system after simply reading the instruction booklet. GPS is perhaps the most important Cold War spinoff that will affect our lives in the future. And I predict every fresh-water angler will take it as much for granted in another year or two as salt-water anglers do today.

If you have an suggestions on how we may improve this Guide or for additional information we can include in future editions, please drop us a line.

Best wishes for tight lines and big fish!
Andy Lightbody

Introduction

When you see the Blue Mesa Reservoir for the first time, if you are not at least a little bit intimidated—you are indeed one heck of a sportsman! The Blue Mesa Reservoir has nearly 100 miles of shoreline and its depths range from 6 feet to over 400 feet. It is angler's paradise, yet remains one tough son-of-a-gun when it comes to ferreting out its angling secrets.

The Blue Mesa Reservoir was built and filled in the 1960's. Since that time, no one one has ever attempted to provide any sort of definitive guide on fishing it! Unless you are an old timer in the area, or can persuade a veteran angler to point you to the proper fishing spots, you will always miss half the fun of fishing one of Colorado's great resources—the largest lake in the state. It is my intent to tell you in this volume where and how to fish the Blue Mesa, and explain what lies both above and below these steely blue waters.

The Blue Mesa Reservoir draws upwards of one million visitors a year and is one of the fastest growing recreational areas in the United States. Summer boating opportunities are fantastic. There are no severe storms to plague outdoor recreationists as on many other western lakes of this class. Waters of the Big Blue contain some of the most fantastic angling opportunities that any fisherman in search of rainbows, browns, Mackinaw lake trout and Kokanee salmon could hope to find.

Boaters also enjoy virtually limitless opportunities to picnic and hike the shoreline and remote inland locations. Wildlife observers and photographers will see a wide range of animal life from mule deer and Rocky Mountain elk to majestic golden and bald eagles soaring high above the lake. Recreational vehicle travelers will find hundreds of camping areas that range from the most primitive to the most sophisticated. Tourists will find a host of hotels, restaurants, guides/outfitters, shopping, gasoline stations, sporting goods stores, and plenty of recreational rental facilities—rafts, horses, and marinas staffed with genuinely friendly people who are glad that you stopped for a visit in Gunnison River Territory !

The nicest thing about writing a guide to the recreational opportunities on the Blue Mesa Reservoir is that it will never be complete. Trophy fishing areas move and new and yet undiscovered areas will be located, and as more people discover the charm of the Blue Mesa Reservoir—new recreational opportunities are sure to develop.

Blue Mesa Reservoir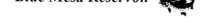

Catching Fish on the Blue Mesa Reservoir

"Fish bite on what fish want to bite on, when they want to."
Andrew Schmitt, Angler, 1965

My grandfather's tackle box had a hodgepodge of terminal tackle in it when I inherited it some 30 years ago. It was a combination of heavy braided lines, hooks, a few surface plugs and lures, various lead weights, some crude feather jigs and flies and more hooks! For Andrew Schmitt, it was all he ever needed to catch more than his fair share of fish.

Open my father's tackle box today, and not much has changed. The heavy braided line has been replaced by spools of monofilament, the plugs, lures, jigs and flies reflect a higher degree of craftsmanship, but always present are the tried and true hooks and lead weights. A lot of the modern lures, jigs and flies that I've given to Dad, are still in his tackle box in unopened packages. I think he hangs onto them so as to not insult me. However, when it comes to fishing, he has favorite baits and lures, they work, and he too has caught more than his fair share of fish!

For the modern angler, walk into just about any store that sells sporting goods today, and you'd have to wonder how the early pioneers and anglers ever survived or gave thought to fishing. How did they survive without Gortex tents, wonder fiber sleeping bags, Coleman camping stoves and lanterns, Mylar space blankets, or freeze dried foods? To compound this ageless mystery, comes questions about how could early pioneers have ever angled for trophy trout without composite fly rods, miracle baits, sinking/floating fly lines, fish finders, temperature gauges, neoprene waders, sunscreen lotions, hand-tied high-tech flies, wonder lures, strike indicators, environmentally friendly fishing weights, belly boats, and Global Positioning Satellite (GPS) receivers?

Ask a lot of old-time anglers, and they'll tell you that 99% of the fish catching lures are designed to catch anglers. If they catch fish, that's a bonus.

While there may be a certain amount of truth in that—especially if you look into any one of my nine fresh water fish tackle boxes marked as "bait," "spin," "fly," "jigs," "lures," "weights," "line," "leaders," etc., I can tell you that unlike the old-time angler, my fishing successes are equally impressive.

"Time" is everyone's biggest enemy today. Gone are the days when most fishermen and fisherwomen really "know" the areas that they are fishing. For Dad and Grandpa, they knew the waters they fished on a regular basis, and they fished them regularly. However, with the advent of high-speed travel—planes, trains and automobiles—have opened up a host of angling opportunities that are very different than fishing the "favorite spots" back home.

My Dad still talks about fishing trips where he and friends spent two weeks fishing certain lakes where the trophy fish were found in abundant numbers. Two weeks and they still did not land a monster Muskie. Today, most anglers do not know what it is like to be able to spend two full weeks learning a prime angling area. Today, if we get three to five days at a time on the water, we consider ourselves fortunate.

We must rely on the local experts who know the area where we are headed, articles we've read in magazines and books, on high tech gear, and on a host of "suggested" lures, flies, baits, jigs and spinners touted as proven fish catchers. Maybe that's why just about any and all dedicated anglers have up to a dozen or more tackle boxes. After all, you never know when that great warbling diving cockroach sinker lure that caught Brookies in West Virginia will work equally well in Gunnison River Territory.

Regardless of how much time you have to spend on the Blue Mesa Reservoir each year, there is a lot of "specialized" tackle that's available to help cut down on the "learning curve."

A great deal of fishing success depends on being in the right place at the right time. But you must also have the right bait to tempt that trout or salmon! Therefore, it is imperative you also know your fish.

Blue Mesa Reservoir

The following paragraphs describe the various species of fish you will find in the Blue Mesa Reservoir.

Rainbow Trout

Although the Blue Mesa Reservoir lies less than 20 miles from one of Colorado's major hatchery's—the Roaring Judy at Almont—the bulk of it's rainbow trout plants come from the Federal trout hatchery in Hotchkiss, Colorado. This is part of the agreement the state has with the Bureau of Reclamation. As a result, over 800,000 fingerling fish are released annually into the waters of the Blue Mesa Reservoir.

Unlike Kokanee salmon which often school together, rainbow trout are much more independent and often scatter to the rock shoals, ledges, bank cuts and other hiding areas that abound on the Blue Mesa Reservoir.

When released into the Blue Mesa Reservoir during the late spring of each year, the fish are only about 5 inches in length. By the end of the summer, they will usually have grown into the 8-10 inch range, and for those that make it through the season and last through to the following year, they will average 14-17 inches or more. These trout have a relatively short life-span of about 2.5 years on average—which helps account for the Blue Mesa's active stocking program.

Rainbows in the Blue Mesa and the lower part of the Gunnison therefore are stocked fish. There are however some native populations that do travel back up into the Gunnison River and some of the larger creeks to spawn. However that percentage when compared to all the rainbows taken by anglers throughout the year is extremely small.

Rainbows are a favorite of boat and shore angler, spincasters, worm drowners and trollers. Virtually all of the time-proven trout catching baits, lures and spinners, as well as some of the new high-tech gizmos, work well on the Blue Mesa.

For shore anglers, bait fishing is a top rainbow producer. Favorites include Berkley floating Power Baits, red worms, nightcrawlers, meal worms, Velveeta Cheese, salmon eggs, crayfish tails and marshmallows. Most popular rigs are spincast rods and reels that are loaded up with light monofilament line. Favorite line weights are in the 4-6 pound test range. Best rigs are ones where the fishing weights are kept small and light, the hooks are small and the angler can keep enough tension on their lines in order to feel even the gentlest "nibble."

Rainbows are famous for "nipping" at the bait, often stripping worms or Power Bait without giving the angler a chance to set the hook. Being able to determine when is the "exact" time to set the hook only comes with lots of practice. Rarely do first time anglers successfully hook and then land each fish that bites, and only plenty of fishing time is going to turn the neophyte angler into the trophy trout taker!

Both shore and boat anglers can also do very well with lures, jigs and spinners. Small Rapala floaters, Rebels and other "fish" lures are good choices. Favorite patterns on the Blue Mesa are small rainbow trout, black and orange, green and orange, silver with orange, and blue with silver. For the spinner angler, Mepps, Fox Creek, Rooster Tails, Panther Martins are good choices. In addition, don't forget small silver or gold Kastmasters, Crocodiles, and spoons. If you're familiar with the bubble-and-fly rig, it can be extremely productive when fished near rock outcroppings and boulder- strewn peninsulas.

Since German Brown trout and rainbows often share the same basic territory, the angler will do best to work the rocks, ledges, boulders, underwater structures, gravel bars and peninsulas where there is good cover and plenty of hungry fish.

Trolling anglers can use both monofilament and lead-core line to help get down in the medium depth waters where the rainbows often congregate. In addition to the favorite spinners and lures, good choices for rainbows include Dick Nites, Arnies, Bubz-Baits, Needlefish, and Tasmanian Devils.

A favorite technique for trollers is to have two to four rods in the water at all times. When working in close to shore, set one or two rods closest to the shoreline with spinners or shallow water jigs on monofilament lines. The other rods should troll in the deeper waters, often with lead-core line to a depth of from 2-3 1/2 colors (8-14 feet). Trolling at speeds where the engine is set at just above the "idle" speed (3-4 miles per hour) is the best bet. Set the drag tight enough on your reels so that even a gentle strike will result in a hooked fish, but loose enough so that line will sound an "audible alarm" when a fish strikes.

Even though there are over 800,000 rainbow trout planted in the Blue Mesa Reservoir each year, the total percentage of fish caught by anglers is less than 15% rainbows. So where do all the rainbows go? Many fall prey to predators long before reaching "catchable" size. Small rainbows are favorite prey for every hunter from hungry shore birds and eagles to large Brown trout and lunker Lakers.

Brook Trout

Mention the words, "brook trout" to the dedicated trout angler and expect his or her eye's to glaze, tongue to thicken and angling arms to twitch Although these fish are often smaller than a trophy lake trout, a bruiser German Brown or even a tackle-ripping rainbow, brook trout hold a great deal of fascination for fisherman.

Brook trout are native to the area throughout the Gunnison River Territory since 1883. But the brook trout is often found in such great numbers in small high-alpine lakes and streams that their growth has been "stunted." Instead of catching a dozen Brookies twelve to fifteen inches in length and weighing in at one to two pound, the angler winds up with fifty or more fish that have large heads and short bodies (9-12 inches) and weight of less than three-quarter pounds.

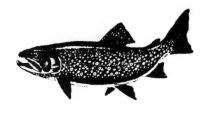

But for the most part in Gunnison River Territory, brook trout are a severely "under-fished" resource! Ask just about any local guide or outfitter, or sporting goods store and they will tell you that there are plenty of areas where anglers can find easy access to great brook trout fishing waters.

On the Blue Mesa Reservoir proper, angler's find few brook trout. For the most part, they stay back in the various Arms that feed into the Blue Mesa, as well as the upper area creeks and streams. Favorite fishing spots for Brookies include the upper parts of Cebolla Creek, Soap Creek, West Elk Creek and even the Lake Fork Arm of the Gunnison.

If you want to find brook trout in the Blue Mesa Reservoir proper, you'll want to drive, boat or hike up to the mouth of the various creeks at the point where they flow into the lake. And they will be there in numbers great enough to satisfy most anglers.

Hike up and away from the Blue Mesa into the Soap Creek or West Elk Creek areas where the topography changes from wide open waters to shallow ponds, pools and beaver dams. The waters may look narrow and shallow, but the fish are often found concentrated there in large numbers. Because the water at these higher altitudes are crystal clear, you can often see the fish lying close to the banks or near underwater banks and fallen tree structures. Keep in mind that if you can see the Brookies, they can see you as well! Whenever you approach any of the ponds or fishable waters, keep a low profile—preferably down on your knees or belly—so you don't alarm the fish.

Fly anglers, spincast and bait fisherman can do equally well on brook trout. Because the fish are often in the eight to twelve inch range, smaller baits, lures and flies are the most productive.

Fly fisherman will do well with both nymphs and dry flies, depending on the local hatch and time of year. Favorites include the mosquito, Prince Nymph, Gray Hackel, Royal Coachman, Orange Asher, Stonefly, blue wing and green wing fly, as well as just about any of the attractor patterns. If you're spincasting, the deadly combination of bubble-and-fly is a top producer. Using a light weight leader on your spincast rod/reel, attach a fly to the end of the line, and approximately twelve to twenty-four inches above this, clip on a clear plastic bobber. It enables the spincast angler to cast the offering like a lure, but retrieve it like a fly fisherman.

Outdoor Life's roving editor, Jim Zumbo, and I had the pleasure of fishing together for brook trout with a bubble-and-fly rig. Both of us finally quit because our arm's got tired of reeling in brook trout! If you think that's an exaggeration—drop him a line at *Outdoor Life* magazine and ask him personally!

For the traditional spincast angler, use the smallest offerings available. Roostertails, Fox Creek Jiglos and Stingers, Mepps spinners, Blue Foxes, are all favorites. If the spinners don't produce top results, have a couple of small one-eighth ounce Gold Kastmasters as a backup. When all else fails, for Brookies, "Kastmasters are my friend," says Jon Garfall of Wapiti Outfitters (303-641- 2603). "Even on the days when the Brookies don't want to bite, I'll help my summer fishing clients take limits of fish with this small gold lure!"

Since many of these small pools and beaver ponds have rarely if ever seen the host of exotic baits that are in use today, the bait fisherman should have a good supply of red worms and small nightcrawler worms along. I've fished cheeses, Power Baits and salmon eggs on numerous occasions, but the best results come with the natural baits because the fish are used to seeing them floating downstream on a regular basis.

My personal opinion is if you're used to eating Stoneflies and drowned worms, and suddenly somebody sets a steak in front of you—even though the steak may taste better—you're instincts are going to go with the worms and the bugs!

German Brown Trout

As most dedicated anglers know, the German Brown trout is a trophy species of fish that is not indigenous to the Americas. However, this often illusive fish has been around for over 100 years in the United States and rates as a top trophy that many fisherman will go after on an exclusive basis in hopes of a 5-pounder or more.

German brown trout were introduced into the GRT long before the construction of the Blue Mesa Reservoir. Records vary as to exact dates, but there is a great deal of evidence to show that the German Brown trout first came to the GRT back in the late 1880s.
The earliest documented introduction was in 1893. After that, several additional brown trout Plants were also made.

Unlike the Rainbow trout that require a yearly replenishment of over 800,000 fingerlings to support the species, the German Brown trout are indeed "on their own." In the Blue Mesa Reservoir, if you catch a nice Brown trout, this is a trophy fish that has literally made it to that level "on it's own." In spite of no plantings, the German Brown trout has done extremely well in just about all areas of the Blue Mesa Reservoir, the Gunnison River and surrounding tributaries and creeks.

Rarely will the angler find the Brown trout out in open waters. Instead, this fish is famous for hiding in close to the rocks, along gravel beds and sand bars, as well as rock shoal outcroppings. Randy at Berfield's Stage Stop (907-641-5782) is one of Gunnison's local Brown trout experts. He says, "While there aren't a lot of Browns caught, as compared to Koakanee salmon, these illusive fish are a real favorite of the dedicated angler heading out to fish the Blue Mesa. You may not catch a lot of Browns, but when you do the chances are excellent that it's going to be a big one."

The Colorado state record German Brown trout was caught here in the Gunnison River Territory at the Public Fishing Ponds below the Roaring Judy Fish Hatchery in 1988. The bruiser Brown topped the scales at 30 pounds, 8 ounces. Obviously this fish migrated into the public trout ponds and spent more than a few years feasting on the smaller rainbow trout that could be found in these easy feeding waters.

For the Blue Mesa Reservoir angler, German Brown trout are frequently caught and reported in the 6-10 pound range. Larger fish are often hooked, but equally often are broken off by over-zealous fisherman when the fish are close to shore or the boat. Are 15 pound plus German Brown trout possible in the Blue Mesa Reservoir? Absolutely!

Fortunately for the big German Browns and unfortunately for the angler, fishing for these fish requires some dedicated effort. Rarely will you pick up a "stupid" Brown while trolling for Kokanee salmon in the deep waters. If you're planning on fishing for Browns, it's going to require a dedicated effort and that means fishing close-in to shore working the lake bottom with everything from your jig, spinner and lure from the shallow waters back to the boat, or the shore angler casting to the deeper waters and working back into the shallows.

For both shore anglers and boat fisherman, I've seen the most big Browns taken on lures such as floating or shallow running Rapalas and Rebels, as well as Fry Bugs and Maribou feather jigs topped off with a meal worm or nightcrawler.

Shore fisherman cast their lures out about as far as they can, and then begin a medium retrieve back to shore. Jig anglers with lead-headed Fry Bugs and Maribous let the jig sink slowly to the bottom and then do a bounce-type retrieve where the baited-jig comes up off the bottom, floats forward a foot or so and then is allowed to gently flutter back to the lake's bottom.

Boat anglers can use both Rapala, Storm and Rebel lures equally well while slowly motoring along the "hotspot" shorelines, Cast up as close to shore as possible and expect most hits or strikes to come in the 3-10 foot water levels. If you're going to fish a Maribou or Fry Bug feather jig, cast up on the shoreline and do the "bounce, flutter and pull" technique that we talked about earlier.

It you're fishing from the shore or a boat and are a bait angler, a recently discovered "fish catching technique" is with the use of crawdads—crayfish. If you read the later section on Crayfish in the Blue Mesa Reservoir, it makes sense that everything from the shallow water Rainbow trout to the big Brown are feeding on the late spring and summer supply of crayfish.

Fishing with crayfish is easy, and is a great "secret weapon" for Big Browns. Break off the tails of even big crayfish, and rig them with a simple leadered #6 hook. Above the crawdad—12-18 inches—attach several split-sinkers, a small rubber-core or an egg sinker. This will give you the weight to cast out from the shore, or back in close to the shoreline if you are a boat fisherman. Either way, allow the crawdad tail to sink to the bottom and retrieve the bait slowly. Because Brown trout work the shallow gravel beds and rock drop offs, getting your bait down to where the fish are is a lot more important than a fast retrieve.

Bait—because fish feed upon it—is a major "plus" in terms of being an attractor. Working crayfish tails by bouncing them along the bottom can be a top producer. If you are looking for a good supply of crayfish bait stop at Gunnison Sporting Goods, the Elk Creek Marina, the Lake Fork Marina, Gene Taylors Sporting Goods or Berfield's Stage Stop. When lures and jigs can't attract the big Brown trout into biting, a bag or two or crayfish tails is a great insurance policy for putting some hungry trout on the stringer!

Mackinaw Lake Trout

Mackinaw Lake trout are a popular species in many large lake and reservoir areas throughout the United States. Head up into Canada or into many of the northern Mid-Western states, and lake trout are a popular winter and summer species for anglers in search of "big trout." In the Blue Mesa Reservoir, fish-planting records show that the Mackinaw lake trout, or Laker, is a rather recent introduction. Final plants of small or fingerling Macs in Big Blue, took place in 1992 and since then the fish have continued a natural population increase by spawning.

Today, the Blue Mesa Reservoir rates as a top Mackinaw fishery. In the late spring months, the prime fishing times are just after the ice comes off of the reservoir. Moderate success can be achieved for those anglers who head to the deeper waters and fish when the Blue Mesa is frozen to a depth of three feet or more from the Lake City Bridge down to the Blue Mesa Reservoir dam. In the late summer, the Blue Mesa's Mackinaw bite seems to all but disappear. Macs move to the deeper waters (80 to 120 feet or more) and are not as responsive as when in shallower waters.

Fish finders and fish graphs often show these deep water "bruisers" are still there, but for some reason, as the water levels and temperatures in the reservoir increase, the "bite" slows. Some anglers will tell you that the Mackinaws are still there and hungry, but many anglers turn their attention to the other trout species which are more plentiful and whose limits are more generous.

Mackinaw fishermen on the Blue Mesa Reservoir are a small and select group. And often tight-lipped about their angling successes. I've spent a few dedicated days fishing Laker hot-spots in late summer and have had very good success. But instead of catching ten fish per day, I consider myself lucky to hook into two or three fish. I've broken off on 17-pound test line that snapped as easily as 2 pound test on a 10 pound Brown trout. When I've told that story, most people respond by telling that I just snagged the bottom. Not that time.

Keep in mind then that late summer Mackinaw fishing is reserved for only the most dedicated.

Favorite fishing lures, tactics and techniques for the Mackinaw lake trout are specialized by comparison to browns, rainbows and even Kokanee salmon.

Mackinaws for the most part are found in deep waters—and angling on the Blue Mesa means that they can be caught from the shoreline, as well as from boats. You stand an equal chance of landing a real lunker with either method.

For the shore angler, the shallower waters—15-30 feet—are where the cruising Macs come in close to shore to feed or when chasing small trout and Kokanee salmon. Anglers in search of a Big Mac Attack need to work the "identified" areas that have proven successful in the past. If you find a new area where the waters start shallow with plenty of trout and Kokes, then drop off steeply, I'd appreciate a personal report so we can include the area in our next book!

Fishing from the shore, Mac anglers will find that these big trout like "fresh meat." Dedicated jig fisherman will swear by the lead-headed tube jig or Gitzit topped off with a large piece of sucker meat. However, bait anglers will say that weighted sucker minnows or large sucker meat offerings are best. For the true bait angler, the best rig is to use either a sliding sinker rig, or a rig where the weight is at the bottom.

Both anglers use the same #1-0 or #2-0 hooks. Sliding sinker anglers will use a 1/2 to 1-ounce "egg" sinker that is held into position by swivels, or even small "split shot" weights approximately 24 inches above the baited hook. This allows plenty of casting weight with which to send the bait out into the deeper depths for the cruising Macs, but allows enough free-travel of the line for the angler to detect a strike or gentle bite.

For the bottom-weight angler, the best bet is to tie a drop-weight in the 1/2 ounce to 1 ounce range at the end of the line. Above that at about 18-24 inches above the weight is tied a short 6-9 inch leadered hook, to which you attach a large minnow or sucker meat offering. Cast out and allowed to settle to the bottom, the weight holds on the bottom with the minnow or sucker meat offering some two feet above. That puts the bait right into the area which large Mackinaws like to cruise as they head up into shallower waters.

For the boat angler, trolling with large spoons and deep diving jigs can be very productive at deep depths. Favorite offerings include Dare Devil spoons, Flatfish, large Rapalas, and Mac Attacks. When fishing the large open waters, keep in mind that the Macs will be in deep—forty, eight or 120 feet of water. Most trolling rigs with standard monofilament lines will have a difficult time getting down to the depths where the large Macs are lounging. Most successful anglers use downrigging devices, or lead-core fishing line at from 6-9 colors. Lead core line will usually carry most lures down four feet for each color of lead-core line extended. However, if you're using a deep diving spoon, Flatfish or other deep diving lure, it's easily possible to troll through the area where the big fish are holding.

Most boat anglers are productive when using lead-headed plastic tube jigs or Gitzits that are topped off with a slice of sucker meat. Gitzits can range from 1/2 to 1-1/4 ounce leadheads, that are then fitted with a plastic "tube jig." Berkley Power Tubes have a built-in natural scent and also work great. Favorite colors include fluorescent white, white, black, orange, smoke, green and Root Beer. Topped off with a strip of sucker meat measuring approximately 1-inch in width and about 2-3 inches in length, the best technique is to literally "bounce" the jig off the bottom when in deep waters.

The ideal day on the Blue Mesa for Macs includes those with calm winds and a smooth surface. If the wind picks up, try to anchor up, or at least let the anchor drag upon the bottom to slow your drift.

When the Laker's bite, let the fish take the bait and don't set the hook too soon. Often times Macs are famous for picking up a baited jig and carrying it in their mouth for 10 yards or more. Give them line to run! Sometimes they'll drop it for a few seconds, and then come back and pick it up again. It's then a minute or so after the second run that you'll be able to set the hook and start the fight that will last a long time to bring the Mac up from the depths.

Whether shore- or boat-caught, the top trophy Mackinaw lake trout are consistently in the thirty-plus pound range. There is little doubt in my mind that a new state record Mac topping thirty-eight pounds now lives in the Blue Mesa Reservoir. It is only a matter of time until some lucky angler finds him or herself in the right place, at the right time to land a new record "lunker laker."

Blue Mesa Reservoir

Kokanee Salmon

Introduced into the Blue Mesa Reservoir soon after it was filled, Kokanee salmon were originally put into the lake as "food" for the Mackinaw lake trout. Instead, these cold water cousins to the sea-going Sockeye salmon, have grown into a major angling resource. In fact, Kokanees now account for up to 75% of all fish taken yearly from Big Blue.

Kokanee salmon are driven to return to their birthplace and spawn. An average of 1 to 1.3 million fingerlings are released into the Blue Mesa annually. Kokanee become sexually mature in 3-4 years and start their spawning runs back into the Gunnison River or the Lake Fork Arm of the Gunnison on the Blue Mesa, the fish change from bright, shiny silver to darker colors. The male's body turns brick red or black, the head green and the lower jaw hooks grotesquely. After this transformation, the fish begin their spawn run back up the rivers. Even though the fish's stomach has shriveled to almost nothing and it no longer feeds in the traditional sense, they become much more aggressive which causes them to "strike" out at flies, lures and jigs placed in front of them.

The annual fall spawning run usually starts by the middle of August and can continue through the first week or so of December. To help protect the Kokanee as an ongoing fishing resource, the Division of Wildlife places special regulations into effect each fall. Throughout the summer, the daily bag and possession limit is ten fish per licensed angler. From September 1 through January 31, the daily bag and possession limit increases to forty fish per licensed angler. In addition, a few areas are open to "snagging"—all waters on the Blue Mesa Reservoir west of the Lake City Bridge at Highway 149 are open to snagging. The most productive areas are in and around the Old Stevens Campground, the Wind Surfing area in the Bay of Chickens and the Lake Fork Arm of the Gunnison.

West from the Lake City Bridge at Highway 149 and all the way up the Gunnison River to Almont (Highway 135) snagging of Kokanees is prohibited from September 1 through October 31st. In addition any Kokanee taken out of the these waters—whether snagged inadvertently or caught on a lure or jig—has to be released. Between October 31st and January 31st, those restrictions are lifted for this area and catching, keeping and even snagging of Kokanees is again permitted.

As you can guess, once the Kokanee salmon makes it back to the hatchery, they are caught and literally milked of eggs and sperm for using in next year's crop of fingerling fish. On average the Roaring Judy Trout Hatchery collect five to ten million salmon eggs during the spawn. After the long spawning run back up the Gunnison, these fish die quickly after spawning. In order to make maximum use of this great resource, the Division of Wildlife sponsors an annual Great Kokanee GIVE-AWAY.

After the fish have been milked for eggs and sperm, the fish (up to forty per angler) are given away FREE OF CHARGE to anyone with a valid fishing license on selected days. The GIVE-AWAY program usually runs from late October through November. Call the Roaring Judy Hatchery in Almont 970 641-0190 for exact GIVE-AWAY dates. The giveaway program usually starts at 8 am and cars are start to line up at 6 am.

When the fish aren't spawning, for the most part they are found in large schools in the deep waters of the Blue Mesa. I've found schools of Kokanee anywhere from ten to ninety feet deep. Time of the year and water temperatures are major determinants. A good fish finder such as the Hummingbird Wide Eye, used in the areas that we've mapped out with the Global Positioning Satellite locations can help you reduce the time spent trolling and increase the time spent time catching! Because Kokanee are often found in large schools, if you get one to bite, you can often go back through the same school, at the same depth and catch more. Many anglers report that once a large school of fish are found and coaxed into biting, it's possible to boat a limit of ten fish in less than 30 minutes!

Until the Kokanee reaches eight to ten inches, they feed primarily on zooplankton (microscopic aquatic animals). After, they start looking for larger food and are much more likely to take baits, salmon eggs, worms, small spinners and lures. As far as favorite Kokanee lures—walk into any of the GRT's area sporting goods stores and you'll find an extensive lineup of colors, patterns and designs. Favorites include Mepps, Dick Nites, The Lake Otter, Arnies, Fox Creek Lures—Jiglos and Stingers, Budz-Baits, Panther Martins, Rooster Tails, Tasmanian Devils, EGB, Needle Fish, Cherry Bobbers, Koke Killers, Kokanee King, Kastmasters, Crocodiles, Rapalas—floating and divers, Rebels, Flatfish, Z-Rays, Blue Foxes, Skinny Minnys, Cripplure, Wedding Rings, and the Mac Special.

Many anglers like to add even more "attraction" to their rigs by using Cowbells and Ford Fenders. Both are heavy monofilament rigs that are attached above the lure and consist of large spinner blades, beads, and directional fins. Some even find that adding a kernel of "white corn" to your lure or spinner is a great attractant. I personally find that a bottle of Trout Attractant "juice" from Berkley adds flavor to all lures. Even while trolling, lures that we've smeared with the trout attractant seem to be more productive over untreated lures and jigs.

Since the Kokanees are usually found down deep, it's important to select gear and tackle that can get your lure down to where the fish are schooling. Most anglers will do best with downrigger or lead-core lines that can "sink" the lure into the depths. However, setting up a Koke trolling rod and reel can be an expensive proposition. Gunnison Sporting Goods (303-641-5022) and both the Elk Creek Marina (303-641-0707) and Lake Fork Marina (303-641-0348) provide rental rods on a daily or weekly basis. Believe me, it's well worth the $10 a day rental charge!

If however you are armed only with spinning gear, trolling weights and heavier jigs/lures such as the Mac Special can help you get down to where the fish are. Use monofilament line in the 10-12 pound test range, with a 6-pound monofilament leader of at least 3 foot length. Using small snap-swivels or barrel swivels are a good way to keep the line from getting tangled, knotted and twisted.

19

Shore anglers will take very few Kokanee salmon. Part of the reason is that Kokanees are down in deeper and colder waters of the Blue Mesa which are difficult for the shore fisherman to reach. However, some bait anglers do well from boats by vertically jigging through a stationary school of fish. Hey, if it was easy, it wouldn't be any fun!

Crawdads

Few anglers, visitors and boaters are aware of it, but Blue Mesa Reservoir is also home to a very large and healthy population of Crawdads, also known as Crayfish. Few are caught on a regular basis by anglers using bait but they are easily captured in homemade or commercial crayfish traps.

These traps that are often little more than aluminum and chicken wire containers that are loaded with fish guts, dog food, bread, stew meat, chicken parts or bacon. Placed near rock outcroppings, it is possible to catch hundreds of these little fresh water lobsters a a day!

Crawdads are popular with the fishy denizens of the Blue Mesa Reservoir as well. The stomachs of German Browns and rainbows are often so full of crawdads that they look as if they are ready to explode. If you use them for fishing, break off the tail section. Although the crayfish will often reach five to six inches in length, only the tail seems to be the best "bait." Use small hooks with light monofilament line and just enough weight to sink the crayfish tail, then expect some excellent fishing.

If you like shrimp or lobster, you're going to love Blue Mesa Reservoir crawdads. To make a meal of them, you need at least 20-25 crayfish per person. Any of the good commercial "Crab Boil" products from the Gunnison Safeway or City Market will help you boil up pounds of these tender delicacies. After they have cooked, simply break off the tail, remove the meat (about one inch long) and dip in melted butter with a splash of fresh lemon juice.

There is no limit on crawdads. Once cooked, the tails can be frozen for later eating and will keep for months in well-sealed freezer bags. Believe me, even if the fish aren't biting, the crawdads in mid-to-late summer can be found by the thousands. It's probably one of the best-kept culinary secrets of the Blue Mesa!

Navigating The Blue Mesa Reservoir

The Blue Mesa Reservoir lies at an altitude of 7,519 feet.

Information about the Currecanti Recreation Area?
Tune your radio to 1610 AM.

Global Positioning System Reference Check
N 38º   32.666 W 106 º 55.611
(Downtown Gunnison)

On a body of water as large of the Blue Mesa Reservoir, simple sketch maps and vague directions are of little help to the angler. How many "honey-holes" have you been directed to by local experts: "3 miles down the County road, then turn left on the first dirt road past the Miller Ranch, then take a left on the trail where the big tree was five years ago that got struck by lightning."

    1) I don't know what County Road you're talking about?

    2) Where the heck is the Miller Ranch?

    3) I wasn't here five ago when a big tree was struck by lightning. Most fishing guides are not a great deal of help in locating the best spots: ". . . from this intersection downstream to Mogote is the most popular section of the river and access is very good . . . the trees are lined with cottonwood and occasional piñon and juniper and the deadfall from these is . . . ." Where the heck is Mogote and how far away from it is this spot? Trying to get clear, concise instructions on locating a prime fishing hole or even a good camping spot is often just as tough as trying to hook into a tight-lipped trout.

    There's little question that the Blue Mesa Reservoir has a host of "secret spots" that have yet to be discovered. So we have not only listed a host of our prime fishing areas, but have pinpointed them, thanks to the world of the high technology and the Global Positioning System, an American military project spear-headed by the U.S. Air Force which has placed a total of 24 satellites into orbit to provide our troops with their exact location anywhere in the world within ten feet! The system proved itself during the Persian Gulf War and with the Cold War receding into history, the GPS system is available to everyone to use.

What Is GPS?

GPS, or the Global Positioning System, is the new buzz word in the outdoors. But what exactly is GPS and what benefit does it offer fishermen, hikers, boaters, and other outdoor sportsmenand sportswomen?

GPS consists of a constellation of satellites deployed by the U.S. government that orbit the Earth twice a day. These satellites continually transmit precise information on time and their location. Using GPS receivers, people can determine their latitude and longitude by locking onto at least three satellites, and their altitude by locking onto four.

This navigation information allows hikers to establish their own electronic trails. Campsites, trailheads, remote lakes and other destinations can be recorded in the receiver's memory and then later recalled to find the quickest, most convenient route to them. You can use the position, tracking and navigation features of GPS receivers while fishing, canoeing, kayaking, mountain biking and climbing, off-road rallying, snowmobiling, cross country skiing, and orienteering—to name just a few activities.

For example, boaters and anglers can use the system to return exactly to their favorite fishing areas. Hunters, hikers, 4-wheelers or anyone who ventures into the wilderness can also use GPS to find their way home or locate previously identified sites. Bad weather, unfamiliar terrain and darkness no longer prevent hikers from knowing where they are or getting to where they want to go.

In addition to telling you your current position, GPS can graphically show you the distance and direction to your destination, how fast you are moving, and your estimated time of arrival. Most GPS receivers will store hundreds of locations in memory.

Most GPS receivers also have a "backtrack" feature that allows users to mark their route into the wilderness with a series of electronic "breadcrumbs" then re-trace their steps to return. The procedure may sound complex, but it's easily done with just a few keys and a user-friendly menu. For many who have already "locked on" to the GPS technology, they have found that it's easier to use a GPS receiver than to program a VCR.

Magellan Systems, one of the leading manufacturers of GPS receivers, makes this new age navigation especially convenient with its line of portable GPS receivers. The Trailblazer XI is a popular model that weighs 14 ounces and fits easily into the palm of your hand. It was designed to be carried conveniently in a backpack, pocket, glove compartment or tackle box.

In addition to the standard navigation information, the Trailblazer XL has an easy-to-read Graphical Track Plotter that depicts the history of the route that has been traveled. Another screen shows a Trip Odometer that indicates the number of miles that you have traveled. Other screens show which satellites in the GPS constellation are overhead, and a "Moon Phase" screen graphically shows the moon phase for any date as well as sunrise and sunset times.

The XL is waterproof and powered by only three AA alkaline batteries. It will run for up to six hours in continuous operation or for days if used intermittently. An optional mounting kit can be used to power the unit from a 12 volt external source such as a truck or boat battery.

The best news yet is that GPS technology is now available for less than the cost of many sporting goods items such as backpacks, fishing tackle, optics and some outdoor clothing. As the technology improves in the future, GPS receivers will continue to shrink in size and price.

Now, the worldwide availability of GPS allows outdoorsmen to venture into unfamiliar territory from Colorado to Pennsylvania, or from Canada to Africa, and still have the ability to go from camp or truck into the wilderness and back again. Even on familiar turf, GPS allows you to go deeper into the woods for greater solitude and more exciting exploration. For more information, contact Magellan Systems Corporation at 1-800 707-5221.

Magellan Systems Corporation

Using the GPS System

Using a simple hand held receiver, such as the Magellan Trailblazer—the one we used while mapping and to record our favorite fishing locations—I guarantee that you will boat or hike back to a specific location every time.

The GPS system is so accurate that anyone and everyone with a GPS receiver will be able to find or locate a fishing area to within 100 feet. Dozens of times, using the GPS receiver, I have found my way back to the same remote, hard-to-reach area for a fine afternoon of fishing. And don't think that the GPS receiver is only for fishermen. Many people are lost every year in the mountains and deserts because they have trouble reading a map and pinpointing their location. With a hand-held GPS receiver, you will never be lost again, whether you are crossing the Arctic icecap or hiking in the deepest wilderness.

For those of you who don't yet have a GPS system receiver, we've also included traditional camping and fishing hotspot information in terms of highways traveled, distances and mile markers. We've also included a map with the latitude and longitude indicated. So, whether you are armed with a sophisticated GPS receiver or map, you will be able to find your way around the Blue Mesa Reservoir to the best fishing, camping and recreational opportunities with this guide.

Magellan GPS units in Gunnison River Territory are available at **Cottonwoods** and **Gene Taylor's Sporting Goods Stores** (see directory section). Both have set up unique "day rental" programs for anglers and outdoorspersons to not only see and test the GPS units, but to take them into the field for actual use. Costs are about $15.00 per day, and are secured with a major credit card. This is a great way for boaters and anglers to learn about and enjoy the benefits of the GPS system when they want to find an "exact location" for great fishing today—and for tomorrow! The way the trend in GPS popularity is gaining, the traditional compass will soon be found only in antique shops before the end of the decade. If you want access to all the prime fishing and camping locations throughout the Gunnison River Territory, make sure you set your GPS receiver to:

N 38º 32.666   W 106 º 55.611

On the map, that translates to the main downtown intersection of Gunnison, Colorado. If you don't yet have a GPS receiver, we have also provided map directions and they translate to Highway 50, which runs east to west and is named Tomichi Blvd within the city limits, and the intersection with Main Street (Highway 135 north to Crested Butte).

Blue Mesa Reservoir

Great fishing is like finding gold. It's where you find it.
If it was so easy, we'd change the words, "gone fishing," to "gone catching."

Everything from the weather to water level to your skill as an angler, the time of day and the state-of-mind of the local fish effect the overall success of a daily fishing trip.

All that said, being "armed" with information about specific areas about where-to-go, and then how-to catch the fish will cut down on a lot of "legwork." Why waste valuable time searching when you could be fishing and catching?

For the angler, camper and other outdoor recreational users, the following information should be a valuable guide in planning visits to the Gunnison River Territory.

What You Should Know
Blue Mesa Reservoir is twenty miles long and consist of three large basins which are, from east to west, Iola, Cebolla (See Vol Ah) and Sapinero. All three offer excellent fishing and vast expanses for boating. The lake opens up unexpectedly into narrow arms which wind back into the hills offering boaters peace and privacy. Many will take you to areas otherwise inaccessible by hikers. Launch ramps are located at Elk Creek, Lake Fork, Iola and Steven's Creek.

But the boater should be aware that you are high in the Rocky Mountains and that in late afternoon particularly, strong winds can blow up with little notice. *Be Alert*. When the winds do come up, head for shore immediately.

Federal and state boating regulations apply. Your boat must be registered in Colorado or in your home state. You must carry all Coast Guard-Approved floatation devices for each person aboard. You must also carry a bailing bucket, paddle or oar, fire extinguisher, tools to make minor repairs and anchor and line. we also suggest that you always carry warm jackets, no matter the time of year or the condition of the weather when you started out.

Angling Guide to the

Federal park rangers patrol the Blue Mesa Lake. They will help boaters in trouble and they are always on the lookout for infractions of boating rules. They will be happy to check your boat and your safety equipment on request.

You should know the "rules of the road"—posted at all launching sites. Know what to do in case your boat overturns. Keep well clear of spillways. Maintain a watch at all times for flags signaling that divers are below—a red square with a white diagonal stripe. Give them plenty of room. If you tow water skiers when not devoting your time to other worthwhile pursuits, like fishing, do not tow skiers within 500 feet of beaches or mooring areas, or within 100 feet of swimming areas or swimmers. Do not allow anyone to ride on the bow of your boat—it is both dangerous and illegal.

When trolling, always keep a watch ahead for traffic or obstructions. When casting, do so only while seated. When netting fish, do so slowly and calmly so that you do not rock the boat.

Colorado Fishing Rules, Regulations and Limits

If you're planning on fishing the Blue Mesa Reservoir and are over the 15 years of age, you need a valid Colorado fishing license and it must be in your possession. If you are 14 years of age or younger, or there are young anglers in your fishing party, a fishing license is not required for them. The daily take and total possession limits for under 15 anglers is one-half the adult limits. However, anglers under 15 who purchase a fishing license—season, daily, etc.—are entitled to the same bag and possession limits as adult anglers.

Here are the basic rules and regulations that will keep you from getting ticketed by patrolling Department of Wildlife officers.

1)   The general fishing license issued by the state of Colorado is valid from January 1 to December 31st of the same calendar year.

2)   Licenses are available for both resident and non-resident season anglers. If you can prove that you have been a resident of the state of Colorado for the previous six months, your license will cost appreciably less than for the non-resident angler.

3)   If you are a non-resident angler, or even a resident who fishes on an occasional basis, then 1 and 5 day fishing licenses are available.

Blue Mesa Reservoir

4) Free licenses are available for disabled Veterans.
5) All anglers planning to fishing with more than one rod must have a "second rod stamp."
6) In general, the daily total "bag "limit, is the same as the total "possession limit." This means that if you catch your limit of trout on the first day, you can't go back and catch another limit of fish the next day. However, if you have a "trout fry or cookout after leaving the water, and consume all the fish you caught, you are eligible to catch and have in your possession a full bag limit of fish to take back home. As this is written, the basic trout fishing regulations for the Blue Mesa Reservoir require that both the daily bag and total possession limits are 8 trout, total. This includes a combination of both Brown trout and rainbow trout. The only exception at this writing are Mackinaw lake trout. There is little question that the Mackinaw lake trout population in the Blue Mesa Reservoir is exploding. At present, the limit is 1 Mackinaw per day, with 1 Mackinaw in possession. In addition, any fish in the "slot limits" that measure over 22 inches but under 34 inches must be returned to the water immediately. Expect that to change in the near future as the DoW revises it's slot limit limitations and greatly increases the daily bag and possession limits. Check with the DoW "regs" for the most current rules and bag/possession limits. See Appendix C for addresses and phone numbers.

   For the Kokanee salmon fisherman, you can not only take your limit of 8 Rainbow and Brown trout combined, but you can also take 10 salmon during the regular fishing season. On the Blue Mesa Reservoir in the designated areas where snagging is permitted from September 1st through January 31st, that limit increases to 40 fish per day by angling or snagging and in total possession. Several of the major creeks that feed into the Blue Mesa Reservoir hold large resident populations of brook trout. If you fish both the Blue Mesa Reservoir and a major feeder creek, you can take up to 10 brook trout as well.

7) To make certain that you are in compliance with all the rules and regulations that govern the Blue Mesa Reservoir, make sure that when you purchase your fishing license that you also secure a

copy of the Colorado Fishing Season Information and Wildlife Property Directory. Read it to familiarize yourself with all the regulations and make sure that you toss a copy of this booklet into your tackle box.

8) If you are not an angler and therefore do not need to purchase a Colorado fishing license, you may want to consider spending a few dollars to invest in a basic "Outdoor   Certificate. "The Outdoor Certificate has been called the "cheapest outdoor insurance policy available. This certificate will ensure cost-free search and rescue services in the event that you become lost, your vehicle or boat breaks down, you become injured or run into any other out door emergency requiring rescue services from local, regional, or state authorities.   Without the Outdoor Certificate, fishing, hunting or other recreational license, you can be liable for up to hundreds of thousands of dollars in rescue effort costs.

Navigational Aids

Recognize and obey the navigational flags, listed below.

Diamond Shape, red border, white interior: DANGER. USE CAUTION

Square, red border, white interior: INFORMATION

Diamond, red borders with red cross: DANGER. KEEP OUT

Red Square with white diagonal: DIVERS BELOW

Red Bouy: KEEP RIGHT WHEN MOVING UPSTREAM, LEFT WHEN MOVING DOWNSTREAM

Black Bouy: KEEP LEFT WHEN MOVING UPSTREAM, RIGHT WHEN MOVING DOWNSTREAM

Striped bouy—Right: CHANNEL MARKER, KEEP RIGHT

Stripped bouy—Left: CHANNEL MARKER, KEEP LEFT

Angling Guide to the

Best Bets For Angling And Camping On The Blue Mesa Reservoir

We've made it as easy on you as possible! Listed below are the best fishing sites so far discovered on the Blue Mesa Reservoir. We have tested each location several times and the comments are our personal opinion, often supplemented by those of local anglers.

Each site is located for you by directions along and in relation to Highway 50, the main east-west axis on the Western Slope. In addition, we have provided the GPS coordinates for each location to within thirty yards. Where possible, we have also listed a telephone number. You can't miss.

Where to Fish the Blue Mesa Reservoir

We've divided the Blue Mesa Reservoir into five main sections simply because it is too big to try and describe as one entity. They are: Gunnison River Approach, Iola Basin, Cebolla Basin, Sapinero Basin, Morrow Point Reservoir and Lake Fork Arm.

Our recommended angling spots are then described in a counterclockwise rotation around the basin. For instance, in the Iola Basin, we started at the Lake City Bridge and went east along the north shore, then over to the south shore and east again along the south shore to the Lake City Bridge once more.

It may sound confusing but it is not when you look at the map included between pages 26-27. Just remember that we are working counterclockwise around each of the five areas. Since we have given the longitude and latitude for every location, you need only refer to the map or your GPS receiver to find the spot you are reading about.

Gunnison River Approach to the Iola Basin

I1   **Gunnison's Twin Bridges,** 1.5 miles west from downtown on Highway 50
      N 38o 31.960 W 106o 57.031
West on Highway 50 (1.5 miles from downtown). Located near the Dos Rios municipal water plant, there's public access to over 1/4 mile

30

of the Gunnison River. Ideal for spin and fly anglers who like to walk and wade. The area is also a popular spot for putting in and taking out river rafts and kayaks. No camping facilities at this location, but a great spot for day use that's close to town.

I2   **Mesa Campground,** 4 miles west from downtown on Highway 50 (970-641-3186)
     N 38º 31.332 W 106º 59.423
Located 4 miles from downtown on West Highway 50, Mesa Campground is the last commercial operation before entering the Curecanti Recreation Area. In addition to a newly renovated convenience store, they have tackle, licenses, RV and tent sites, propane, showers and gasoline.

I3   **Country Road 32,** 4.5 miles west from downtown on Highway 50 (153 mile marker)
     N 38º 31.281 W 106º 59.722
Access route to the Riverway Day-Use Campground

I4   **Riverway Campground,** 2/10ths mile down County Road 32
     N 38º 31.119 W 106º 59.700
Riverway Campground provides shoreline/streamside fishing on Gunnison River. Campground is for day use only, no overnight camping. Campground has large picnic area, Bar-B-Qs, and restrooms. Area is popular "take-out" point for Gunnison River rafters.

I5   **Neversink Day Camping Area,** 6 miles west from downtown on Highway 50
     N 38º 30.974 W 107º 01.104
Neversink Campground provides excellent access to shoreline and streamside fishing on Gunnison River. Area also provides gentle hiking trails. Campground is for day use only, no overnight camping. Campground has large picnic areas, Bar-B- Qs, and restrooms. River access at this location is known for excellent Kokanee salmon fishing in the late summer when the fish begin their spawn migration out of the Blue Mesa Reservoir and back up Gunnison River. Check regulations in regards to snagging for salmon, and closed season dates.

I6 **Cooper Ranch Day Camping Area**, 6.5 miles west from downtown on Highway 50
N 38o 30.607 W 107o 01.542

Cooper Ranch Campground area provides excellent access to shoreline and streamside fishing on the Gunnison River. Area also provides a host of gentle hiking trails. Campground is for day use only, no overnight camping. It has large picnic areas, Bar-B-Qs, and restrooms.

I7 **Beaver Creek Day Camping Area**, 8 miles west from downtown on Highway 50 (150 mile marker)
N 38o 29.664 W 107o 01.878

Daytime fishing access on Gunnison River or Blue Mesa. Nicely wooded campground for day use only, no overnight camping. Access to the river is via an underpass that runs under Highway 50. Campground has picnic areas, Bar-B-Qs, and restrooms. River access is in location where the waters often run fairly fast and open. Great spot for the walk/wade fly fisherman or spin-cast angler

I8 **No Name Turnout**, 8.5 miles from downtown
N 38o 29.378 W 107o 02.325

This turnout has no "official name" but it's a great spot to pull off the highway and drive down to the edge of the Gunnison River where it widens out nicely. Waters are relatively calm and deep in the summer time, and is a favorite area for hungry rainbows. Porta-potties are the only facilities provided. Lots of rafters and small boaters like this area for putting in and taking out.

I9 **Mouth of the Gunnison River At the Lake City Bridge**
N 38o 29.254 to 29.281 W 107o 03.523 to 03.421

The Gunnison River empties into the Blue Mesa Reservoir here and forms a small basin which is easily accessible to anglers. Shore anglers can reach both north and south sides of the Blue Mesa Reservoir via Highway 50 to Highway 149. Shallows on both the north and south sides provide great angling areas for bait fishermen using worms, Berkley Power Baits and other offerings.

Boat anglers will want to stay in the "channel" areas where the currents are constant. Spin and lure casting anglers do well, as well as trolling fisherman.

110   Horizontal Tree
      N 38º 29.274 W 107º 03.390

Located about 500 yards east of the Lake City Bridge and only visible during extremely low water periods, this dead-fall tree provides shelter for numerous trout. A GPS unit will make it easier to find this "secret location"—just home in on the coordinates above for a very productive trout fishing excursion whether you are a spincast angler or bait fisherman. It's inaccessible to shore anglers as it lies nearly 100 yards from the shoreline. For the boat fisherman, this is an under-fished haven for trout in the summer, and a resting place for Kokanee salmon in the fall.

Iola Basin

111   Junction Highway 50 and Highway 149 Commonly called the
      Lake City Bridge, 56 miles to Montrose
      N 38º 29.143 W 107 03.500

NOTE: This junction will take you either further West on Highway 50 towards the Blue Mesa Dam and plenty of more fishing locations, or allow you to turn south on Highway 149 and head towards Lake City where you'll find walking access to the Lake Fork Arm of the Gunnison/Blue Mesa Parking area.

While you're trying to decide which direction to go—don't overlook the excellent fishing found here at the Lake City Bridge area. Both boat and shore anglers will find plenty of rainbow and brown trout action here. There's a small paved pull-out on the south side of the Lake City Bridge on Highway 149, and restroom facilities, as well as a small picnic area.

Boat anglers will do well trolling in and around the Bridge. Between the second and third pillar on the South Side of the bridge is a relatively strong underwater current. Rainbows and browns seem to seek out this current area as it often brings food to them. Drift fish this area with baits, lures and spoons.

In the "bay" that lies just west of the Lake City Bridge, waters in the 15-25 foot depths are where you'll find small to medium-sized Mackinaw Lake trout in the early summer, and often schools of Kokanee salmon (2-3 pound range) in the late summer months.

North shore anglers should fish from the rocks and boulders along Highway 50. Watch out for snags, but a lot of big browns are often found in 10-12 feet of water around these rocks.

South shore anglers will find gentle angles and muddy bottoms. Top spot is right under the bridge back towards both north and south of the cement pillars. Baits are top producers.

I12   **Highway 149 at Sapinero Mesa Road** (County Road 26) Connects Highway 149 to Highway 50 and is often called the **Lake City Cut-off.**
       N 38o 16.854 W 107o 10.581

It's 16 miles at this juncture—via dirt road—back to Highway 50 at the Blue Mesa Reservoir, and 30 miles back to Gunnison. It's a shortcut if you're heading back to Montrose or want to save time in getting back down towards the middle of the Blue Mesa Reservoir.

I13   **Blue Mesa Road,** 24.3 miles up Highway 149 from Highway 50. It's located at the 93 mile marker on Highway 149.
       N 38o 17.618 W 107o 13.119

This is the dirt road turnoff for anglers, campers and hikers that will lead you to both the Red Bridge Campground (located 2 miles down the Blue Mesa Road) and Gateview Campground (located 7 miles down the Blue Mesa Road). Both of these are located on the Lake Fork Arm of the Gunnison River. Both have primitive camping facilities, with 14-day stay limits.

Keep in mind that there are no public fishing areas on the Lake Fork before the Red Bridge. The Campground found at the Red Bridge is operated by the Bureau of Land Management (BLM).

From the Red Bridge Campground down to the Gateview Campground this area is controlled and operated by the National Park Service. This entire 5-mile stretch of the Lake Fork Arm of the Gunnison River is wide open for anglers, hikers, photographers, etc. Look for areas where the River has steep drop offs and deep pools. Rainbows, browns, and even the occasional cutthroat trout like to hole up in areas where the waters are deep, and a little calmer than the main flow of the river. Keep in mind that the water is so clear, that if you can look down and see the fish swimming, chances are excellent the fish can see you too! Keep your shadow and reflection off these clear pools! Favorite angling techniques will include all the standards for fly fishers, spin casters and bait anglers. Colorado Division of Wildlife Officer, Phil Mason says some of the favorites he sees anglers using on a regular basis include small Rapala lures, most all of the popular pattern spinners—including the Gunnison Sporting Goods produced Lake Otter in silver or gold, Fox Creek lures, and Panther Martins. Favorite flies will include just about all the popular attractor patterns. Obviously if there's a "fresh- hatch" of insects in the air, this will have a marked impact on the favorite flies to use. Popular patterns include Prince Nymphs, Wooly Worms, Royal Coachmen, Orange Ashers, and Yellow Humpies. The Lake Fork Arm is described more fully in the Lake Fork Arm of the Blue Mesa Reservoir. See page 68.

If you're going to stay on Highway 50 and are heading west towards Montrose, go past Highway 149 and then look for:

I14 Steuben Creek Pipeline
N 38o 29.334 W 107o 03.606
Located just west of the Lake City Bridge and accessible from West Highway 50, the Steuben Creek pipeline is virtually invisible to both the boat and shore angler without a GPS receiver. The gentle and constant water flows that run into this area on a year-round basis make it a region where rainbow trout like to congregate. In addition to fresh and highly rich oxygenated waters, the pipeline and stream current also supplies constant flow of fresh food for hungry fish. Bait anglers after rainbows and boat fisherman also, will do well with jigs and bait fishing

I15 Rock Shores West of Steuben Creek
N 38o 29.247 W 107o 03.836
This region is just west of the Steuben Creek pipeline on the north side of the Blue Mesa Reservoir and is popular with shore anglers as it holds very healthy populations of brown and rainbow trout. Bait anglers from the shore do well with worms—meal, red, nightcrawlers—as do bait anglers armed with cheese, marshmallows, salmon eggs and Berkley Power Baits.

I16   **Stevens Creek Campground,** 146 mile marker on Highway 50
     N 38o 29.270 W 107o 05.476

On the north shore, the Steven's Creek Campground is a popular summer and fall camping area. It offers both daytime and overnight camping facilities. No RV hook-ups, but paved camping spots that include picnic areas, Bar-B-Q's, and restrooms. In addition the area provides a gravel boat ramp for launching and removing small fishing boats, as well as some very good shore angling areas for bait fishermen.

The area isn't known for trophy trout, but it does provide an easily accessible area for anglers that are looking for some good "pan-sized" trout for the frying pan or the take-home freezer. Best bet baits are going to include just about all of the favorite bottom rigs with sliding sinkers that are used in conjunction with nightcrawler worms, redworms, wax worms, salmon eggs and Berkley Powerbait in a variety of colors and offerings.

I17   **Old Stevens Picnic Area,** 145 mile marker on West Highway 50
     N 38o 29.145 W 107o 06.119

This area offers lakeside daytime camping with picnic tables, BB-Q pits and restrooms. The area also affords some fine shore fishing access to the lake. Shore anglers will do best with salmon eggs, Powerbait, worms, cheeses, marshmallows and other popular trout baits. This area is also popular for Kokanee salmon snaggers in late fall. It is regularly planted with salmon each year which return to spawn from late September into October.

I18   **Sunnyside Campground.** Near the "145 mile marker" on West
     Highway 50,   28357   Highway   50
                                    Gunnison, CO 81230 970
                                    641-0477

     N 38o 29.023 W 107o 06.116

Private camping and RV sites are available on a daily, weekly or seasonal basis. The campground has a convenience store with groceries including fresh milk/ice cream, fishing tackle, licenses, propane. Facilities include coin-operated showers, and laundry facilities, and a public telephone. Long term RV and boat storage is also available.

119 **East Side of the Blue Mesa Ranch Island**
N 38o 28.549 W 107o 06.608

During low water, you can drive out onto the peninsula that it forms. Shore anglers fish both the east and west side of Blue Mesa Ranch Island for German Brown and rainbow trout, and deep waters for Kokanee salmon. When the waters of the Blue Mesa rise, this peninsula turns back into an island.

120 **Blue Mesa Ranch "Island."** Near the "144 mile marker" on West Highway 50 Close to Willow Creek
N 38o 28.934 W 107o 06.814

Follow the dirt road turnoff to the island area. It's easy to see heading both east and west on Highway 50. When the water is low, anglers can actually drive out onto the peninsula. Both the east and west side provide good shore angling. Ideal for float-tube fisherman or those with a small raft that want to paddle around. If water levels are high, it does become an island and provides great close-to-shore fishing for boaters looking for hungry rainbow and brown trout. The area around the island has gravel bars, rock outcroppings, rock cliffs and drop-offs. Good for everyone from the bait angler to the spinner/lure and jig fisherman.

121 **Blue Mesa Ranch Island Cove at Willow Creek**
N 38o 28.459 W 107o 06.802

As a peninsula or an island, Blue Mesa Ranch Island at Willow Creek contains a small cove to the west that provides good cover for trout. Shore anglers should work the area at the northwest corner of the island. Boat anglers have the advantage of being able to navigate the narrow channel and fish the entire west side of the island for browns and rainbows.

122 **Blue Mesa Recreational Ranch.** At the "144 mile marker" on West Highway 50, 27555 West Highway 50 Gunnison, CO 81230 970 641-0492
N 38o 28.858 W 107o 07.237

A private membership recreation ranch and 5-star resort with RV sites, large community building and cabins. Member of the Adventure

Angling Guide to the

Outdoor Resorts and Camp Coast-To-Coast. Public tours are welcome, memberships are available and a host of summer recreation activities are ongoing. Ranch has a full-time activities director on site who organizes a host of evening programs, cooking classes, crafts classes, dances and evening BB-Qs for ranch guests. See special camping offer for all vistors on page 120.

I23   Big Rocks West of the Blue Mesa Ranch Island
N 38o 28.311 W 107o 07.052
Within walking distance of Blue Mesa Ranch Island at Willow Creek are some prominent rocks which are an under-fished resource for shore anglers and boaters looking for Browns and rainbows. Boat anglers are going to have to cast their jigs and lures back to the shoreline shallows, while shoreline fisherman with spinners, small lures and bait can work the banks and shoreline shoals in depths of from 3-10 feet of water.

I24   Rainbow Lake Turnoff. At the "143 mile marker" on West Highway 50.
N 38o 28.397 W 107o 08.670
This dirt road turnoff will take the summer angler to great high alpine lake trout fishing. Rainbow Lake lies 12 miles off of Highway 50 and provides plenty of opportunities for day-time hiking, wildlife watching and exploring. In the fall (August-September) it's a prime location for an easy 2-wheel (car) drive to view the autumn colors, particularly the aspens.

I25   Boulder Shoals
N 38o 27.955 W 107o 07.673
Just beyond easy walking distance from the Blue Mesa Ranch Island at Willow Creek, these rocks run from deep waters up to the shoreline. It's a great spot for boat anglers to cast back along the rocks with jigs and lures for rainbows and German Brown trout.

I26   Big Rocks
N 38o 27.987 W 107o 08.175
This large rock formation is easily located with your GPS receiver using the above coordinates. If you don't have a GPS receiver, move to a point 1/2 mile east of the Dry Creek Campground area. Look south

Blue Mesa Reservoir

directly across the Blue Mesa and find a point opposite Third Cove. These rock cliffs and drop-offs are some of the finest German Brown and rainbow trout waters that any angler could ask for.

I27 Dry Creek Campground Island
N 38o 28.195 W 107o 08.589
Accessible either by boat or afoot, the Dry Creek Campground mini-island is on the east side of the campground area. Look for a "shallow water" warning marker. When waters are low in the springtime, it becomes a peninsula. In the mid to late summer when the waters again rise, it turns into an island and boaters should beware! But at any time, it's a great spot for anglers—boaters and shore fisherman. Trolling anglers do well on trout and Kokanee salmon, and shore fisherman will have no trouble fishing this underwater structure for lots of trout.

I28 Dry Creek Day Camping Area. Near the "143 mile marker," West Highway 50.
N 38o 28.349 W 107o 08.863
Dry Creek has plenty of parking for daytime camping, plenty of picnic areas with tables, restrooms, Bar-B-Q pits and fishing access to the Blue Mesa Reservoir for some excellent shore fishing. Jig and lure fisherman should work the rock outcroppings, and bait anglers should use traditional worms, Powerbait, salmon eggs and other trout baits.

I29 Jumper's Cliffs
N 38o 27.790 W 107o 09.023
These shear cliffs can be seen from both the north and south sides of the Blue Mesa Reservoir but are located on the North side. The cliffs tower some 70 feet or more above the high water areas of the Lake and are a favorite area for Western State College students and the "young at heart" to dive into the cold waters of the Blue Mesa.

When swimmers and adventurous divers are not jumping from the cliffs, the area is a fine fishing area for Rainbows, Browns and Kokanee. The trout angler will see the best results when casting spinners, lures and jigs up close to the rock cliffs. Let them flutter gently down in to the depths. Trolling anglers should work the rocks with spinners and lures that reach the 10-15 foot waters.

I30   No Name Rocks—Opposite Turtle Rock Campground
N 38o 27.822 W 107o 09.559

This large rock outcropping located on the north side of the Blue Mesa Reservoir, just opposite the Turtle Rock Campground area is an extremely under-fished area for German Brown trout and rainbows. Work in close to the shoreline with jigs such as Fry bugs/feathered jigs, or deep diving lures (Rapala Countdowns and Deep Diving Rebels) at the rock outcroppings and you'll find plenty of trout from close to shore out to the 15-20 foot depths.

I31   Elk Creek Cove—East of the Elk Creek Marina
N 38o 27.887 W 107o 09.674

This cove is just around the corner from the Elk Creek Marina on the north side of the Blue Mesa Reservoir. Interestingly enough, it's an uncrowded and under-fished area where large schools of Kokanee salmon and trophy Brown and rainbow trout hang out.

I32   No Wake Zone Elk Creek Marina
N 38o 27.669 W 107o 09.781

The area in and around the Elk Creek Marina is home to everything from large size rainbows and browns to cruising Mackinaw lake trout in search of Kokanee salmon. While most boat anglers race away to what they perceive to be "hot spots," often times some of the areas in and around floating boat docks are great fishing areas.

Angling from the boat docks is prohibited, but the rocks in and around the docks have some great brown trout for jig fishermen. The open waters can provide nice rainbow and Kokanee salmon action, and in the deeper waters out between the buoys of the No Wake Zone, trollers can pick up on Macs, rainbows and Kokanee.

From the shore area in and around the Marina, bait, jigs, lures and even flies are popular choices. Rapala lures, Mepps, Roostertails,

Fox Creek lures, Panther Martins and Fry Bugs topped off with meal or red worms are top producers. Traditional fly fishermen will find that spincast gear with a "bubble-and-fly" rigs will enable you to cast out further into the open waters with the same excellent fish-catching results. Shore anglers with crayfish tails will find lots of good-sized brown trout in the rocks.

I33   **Elk Creek Marina/Elk Creek Visitor Center,** 15 miles from downtown Gunnison, located at the "142 mile marker" on West Highway 50. Visitor Center 970 641-0406. Park Headquarters 970 641-2337
      N. 38º 28.224 W 107º 09.805

This is the site of the National Park Service Visitor Center. It has plenty of day-use and overnight camping facilities. The camping areas feature picnic areas, tables, BB-Q pits, restrooms, potable water, hot-water showers, and lots of shore fishing access. The Visitor Center is open from Mid-May through late September and features a fine museum of the Blue Mesa Reservoir, the Curecanti National Recreation Area and the entire Gunnison River Territory. Stop off and visit this center and pick up the latest maps and information about their numerous summer programs—fly fishing clinics, nature/geology programs, Early Man/Ute Indian archeology, dinosaur history, and much more.

I34   **Elk Creek Marina,** 24830 West Highway 50, Gunnison, CO 970 641-0707
      N 38º 27.655W 107º 09.849

The Elk Creek Marina is a full-service Marina area. There's a public boat ramp for anglers and boaters wanting to launch their own private boats. At the marina you'll find slips that can be rented on a daily, weekly, monthly or seasonal basis. The Marina rents nearly everything, from small skiffs to large pontoon boats, groceries and souvenirs, fishing tackle, licenses, soft drinks and beer. The marina can also provide gasoline for all boaters and anglers needs. Both unleaded regular and pre-mix are available. In addition, they also employ mechanics to make minor marine repairs.

While fishing from the dock area of the marina is illegal, there are plenty of areas for excellent shore fishing. In addition to an abundance of rainbows, browns and an occasional cruising Mackinaw lake trout, the area also provides some very good opportunities to find large schools of cruising Kokanee salmon. Shore anglers do well with all the popular trout baits, jigs, Rapala lures and spinners. Boat fishermen will find action near the rocks and shoreline and by trolling slowly back and forth through the "no-wake" slow speed areas. When you're finished fishing for the day, simply walk back up to the top of the boat ramp/hill and you'll find modern fish cleaning facilities complete with running water and garbage disposals.

I35 **Pappy's Restaurant Overlooking The Blue Mesa Lake.** 24830 West Highway 50 970 641-0403
N 38º 27.922 W 107º 09.836

Pappy's Restaurant is located adjacent to the Elk Creek Marina and provides full food and bar service to hungry anglers and boaters. Open for breakfast, lunch and dinner; dine-in, patio and take-out menus.

I36 **Elk Creek Campground Rocks,** Located between the Camp Area and the Marina
N 38º 27.507 to N 38º 25.592 W 107º 10.231 to W 107º 09957

If you walk west from the Elk Creek Marina, or east from the Elk Creek Campground, you'll find a lot of steep rocks and drop-offs on the Blue Mesa Reservoir. These are excellent waters for rainbows and browns. Bait fishermen will do well with all the traditional baits cast "close-in" from the shore with a traditional sliding sinker rig. Berkley Floating Power baits in orange, yellow or the new fluorescent patterns are top producers as are crayfish tails.. Jig fisherman have to slowly work their Maribous, Dallflies or Fry bugs topped off with meal worms back into the shallows. Spinner anglers will find that Fox Creeks, Mepps, Panther Martins and Blue Foxes are top producers. Any of the small Rapala floaters and sinking Count-Downs are also good choices.

This area is a great place to use the "bubble and fly" fishing method. Use of a clear plastic bubble to provide casting weight, followed by a trailed wet, dry fly or streamer. (See the How-To fishing section for more information on fishing techniques).

Boat anglers have a tendency to want to rush away from the Marina areas in search of prime fish locations and often ignore excellent angling opportunities in the immediate area. These "rocks" and "cliffs" provide a good example of an under-fished resource. All of the baits, jigs and lures that we've talked about for the shore angler are going to work equally well for the boat fisherman.

I37   Turtle Rock Boat Camping Area
N 38o 27.756 W 107o 09.436

On the south side of the Blue Mesa Reservoir and just east of the Elk Creek Marina is one of four boat camping sites found on Big Blue. Accessible only by boat, the camping areas provide "primitive" facilities only. Marked camping areas, restrooms, picnic tables and BB-Q pits are there for boat campers who want a lot of privacy.

I38   Turtle Rock Cliffs
N 38o 27.732 W 107o 09.394

These steep rocks at the Turtle Creek Campground area are accessible by shore anglers from the Campground, or by boat anglers. Small jigs and lures can often find stationary trout in the area. Shore fisherman from the Turtle Creek Campground will find that baits—crayfish tails, worms, cheese, Berkley Power Baits and others—with light weights are best when fished from the stepped ledges.

I39   Gravel Bars of Turtle Rocks
N 38o 27.621 W 107o 09.135

Walk out from the Turtle Creek Campground to the East about 500 yards and you'll find a small outcropping of rocks and gravel bars. If you are boat fishing, continue a gentle drift past the Turtle Rocks area. These gravel bars are favorite haunts for brown trout in the shallow waters. Lure anglers will do well casting up at the shoreline and retrieving shallow-water Rapalas and Rebel lures back toward the boat.

I40   First Rocky Point
N 38o 27.692 W 107o 08.898

If you've got a GPS receiver, this is an easy point to locate. If not, look for a "shallow water" marker on the south side of the Blue Mesa

Reservoir 1/4 mile east of the Turtle Creek Campground. In addition to warning boaters of shallow waters, the shallows should be fished by jig and lure casters, as it is the home of a lot of Browns and rainbows.

I41   First Cove
N 38o 27.707 W 107o 08.846

This small cove past Turtle Rocks on the south side of Big Blue is a good spot for trolling in close to shore with small Rapalas, or working the shoreline with feathered jigs.

I42   Shore Area in First Cove
N 38o 27.729 W 107o 08.851

The shore area at the back of the first cove here on the south side of the lake is a favorite for shallow water angling, and a good spot to get out of the wind when it kicks up.

I43   Brown Bank
N 38o 27.761 W 107. 08.827

On the west side of First Cove is a bank that combines some small rocks and boulders with nice gravel bar areas. Drift through this area or motor very slowly and stay in close to shore. Work jigs and lures towards the bank and retrieve back into the deeper waters.

I44   Kokanee Trolling Area
N 38o 27.839 W 107o 08.869

A popular area where down riggers and lead-core line fisherman troll for schools of Kokanee salmon. Use your fish finder to locate the nearly stationary schools of fish and continue to troll back through them once you get the first hookup. Fish are often found from 10-24 feet deep. If fishing lead core, use 2 1/2 colors up to 6 colors to stay deep.

I45   100 Foot Cliffs
N 38o 27.907 W 107o 08.584

These very steep and very shear cliffs are easy to spot and provide deep water angling. Spinners do well when cast up right up at the rock face. Fox Creek spinners, Mepps and bright lures work well when allowed to flutter down to 15-20 feet depths and retrieved slowly.

146 Second Cove
     N 38º 27.844 W 107º 08.420
Located on the south side of the Blue Mesa, this large cove is almost directly opposite the Dry Creek day camping/picnic area. Stay in close to shore if working for browns and rainbows in the shallows, and out about 50 feet if doing a slow troll for Kokanees.

147 Big Gravel Bank
     N 38º 27.811 W 107º 08.292
When waters are low, you'll be able to easily see the very large gravel bank with lots of sand. It's a great place to work jigs and baits for cruising browns. When the water levels are high, it may not look like much, but take my word for it, it's worth bouncing worm-tipped Fry Bugs, Maribous and Dallflies.

148 Third Cove
     N 38º 27.755 W 107º 08.139
Unlike the previous coves that often have steep cuts at the water's edge, this cove has lots of gravel bars to work for rainbows and browns that are in close to shore.

149 Cowbell Point
     N 38º 27.719 W 107º 08.085
On the east side of the Third Cove is a rocky point that causes numerous Kokanee trollers fits! Each year when the waters a low, this rocky point with a large submerged ledge and steep fall offs is loaded with "snagged gear"—cowbell attractors, lures and strings of lead-core line. It's also a great jigging area for rainbows and browns. Favorites are black, yellow, fluorescent green and orange Fry Bug patterns.

150 Colored Cliffs
     N 38º 27.814 W 107º 07.635
A picturesque area with big rocks and a pine tree-loaded shoreline. Up high, the cliffs sport a variety of colors and are often home to nesting hawks and eagles. This is also a favorite run to troll 2-4 colors of lead core line for Kokanees, while working the shallows along the shore with floating Rapalas and Rebels for trout.

I51   **Boulder Point**
      N 38o 27.728 W 107o 07.635
Prominent rock area where deep waters in the 20 foot range are great for vertical jigging and bait fishing.

I52   **Mud Bottom**
      N 38o 27.700 W 107o 07.459
In this area, the contour of the Blue Mesa begins to rise from deep water into numerous shallow water regions. If trolling for Kokes, it may be time to "shorten" the lead-core lengths. Good fishing still abounds, but the fish are going to be found in the 8-10 foot range.

I53   **Sand Cove**
      N 38o 27.677 W 107o 07.242
A shallow water cove that has lots of sand and gravel bottoms. Work the shore line for trout with jigs and bait, and the open waters with small lures trolled shallow. Lead core line should be no more than 2-3 colors if you're trolling spinners, Arnies, Dick Nites, etc. If trolling lures, any of the sinking lures, Rapala Countdowns and others should get you down to the depth where the fish are cruising without lead-core lines.

I54   **Submerged Rocks**
      N 38o 27.640 W 107o 07.215
Your GPS receiver will be handy in locating this underwater structure. If you can find it, it's home to a lot of trout who like to hang around the sides.

I55   **Old Hay Fields**
      N 38o 27.789 W 107o 06.927
The waters on the south side of the Iola Basin area of the Blue Mesa Reservoir are very, very shallow. If you've got a long shaft engine, keep in mind that much of this area is 3-4 feet deep or less. Before the Reservoir was filled, this area was a hay meadow.

Not much angling action in the shallow areas, but 1/4 mile out from shore, waters are back to the 6-10 foot depths. Shallow trolling for Kokes and trout can be productive.

156 Hay Field Peninsula
N 38º 28.109 W 107º 06.529

Located at the east end of the old Hay Fields, this prominent peninsula has a large boulder formation that runs to the water's edge and continues into the depths where the big trout live. Up close to shore, jig and bait anglers will do well. Move out into the channel half-way between the Peninsula and Blue Mesa Ranch Island and you will find schooling Kokanee salmon in these medium depth waters.

157 Iola Basin Rocks—West
N 38º 28.424 W 107º 06.461

Located just to the West of the Iola Boat Ramp, the Iola Rocks are a favorite for both shore and boat anglers. Shore fishermen do well with weighted baits—crayfish tails, worms, Berkley Power bait, cheeses and even marshmallows. Spin fishermen do well with any of the larger 1/4 ounce spinners—Fox Creeks, Kastmasters and Mepps are top producers. Lure anglers find that shallow running Rapala floaters and Countdown lures cast out from shore and worked from the deeper waters back to shore are good for big browns. Boat anglers are often most interested in the large schools of Kokanee salmon that can be found in the area, but working in and around the rocks can turn up a lot of lunker trout.

158 Iola Boat Ramp, 2.5 miles up Highway 149 from Highway 50
N 38º 28.271 W 107º 05.533

Iola boat ramp is the ideal place to put-in and take-out everything from a small raft or rowboat to a large pontoon or house boat. No charge for use of the ramp facilities (at press time). Daytime use camping facilities include picnic area, Bar-B- Q's, and restrooms.

Good shoreline fishing to both the East and West of the boat ramp. Mud and sandy bottom is found to the East of the ramp and is home to a lot of hungry rainbows in the shallow 8-10 feet of water. Worms, salmon eggs, crayfish tails and Berkley Power Bait are top producers.

To the West of the ramp are large rock outcroppings where big browns are often taken in and around the boulders. Browns often will move from the shallows 5-8 feet out to the deeper waters of 15-25 feet.

Only occasionally taken by shore fishermen, most Kokanee are taken by trolling anywhere in 16-25 feet of water with lead-core lines or down-rigger devices. Cruise at speeds just above slow-idle, and when you get into one fish, expect several lines to "hook-up" all at the same time. Watch out for tangles, but once you've found a school of fish, you can often go back through them again and again!

159 Iola Basin Rocks—East
N 38o 28.586 W 107o 05.475

Here is another prominent set of rock outcroppings located east of the Iola Beach area. Up close, its another great area for shore angling and in-close to shore fishing from a boat for trout in the shallows. Out in the deeper waters trout can be found 100-200 feet from shore, this is also a popular area for Kokanee salmon trollers.

160 Shore Angling, Iola from Highway 149
N 38o 28.552 W 107o 04.919

All along this area—easily accessible from Highway 149 via Highway 50 at the Lake City Bridge—there is plenty of shoreline where you will find prime areas for trout and some Kokanee. Keep in mind that after the Kokanees reach a length of about 10 inches, their main food source of lake plankton no longer completely satisfies their appetites. This is why larger Kokes will feed on everything from small fish to tasty baits. Fishing from shore in these areas can provide a great mixed bag of trout and an occasional fat Kokanee salmon.

Boat anglers will find that large schools of Kokanees will increase in numbers throughout the summer in this area. Many spend from late spring to late summer congregating in these area at depths of 10-25 feet in preparation for their fall spawning migration run back up the Gunnison River. Prime fishing months are late June to late September.

161 Iola Basin, Shallows
N 38o 28.728 W 107o 04.387

In what many term the "mother of all Kokanee salmon trolling areas," Iola Basin is probably the most famous area of the Blue Mesa Reservoir for anglers searching for these two pound plus fish. Thousands and thousands of salmon congregate in these waters during the summer months and are catchable at depths from 10-20 feet.

162   Iola Basin, Deep Waters
N 38º 29.098 W 107º 03.908

When great numbers of Kokanee salmon fill the shallows in this area, many of the schools are forced into the deeper waters of Iola Basin. Even though some of the water depths may be in excess of 40-70 feet, the fish will often be found congregating in the 10-30 foot depths. Use your fish finder to locate these large schools, or troll your down riggers or lead-core lines at varying depths. Lead core anglers will find plenty of fish in the 3-5 color depths. Spinners and lures trolled through the area are top producers.

163   Pylon Channel At the Lake City Bridge
N 38º 29.253 W 107º 03.593

After crossing the Blue Mesa Reservoir to the south side on the Lake City Bridge (Highway 50 to Highway 149), count back to between the third and fourth pylon from the south shore. This is the "action channel" where some exceptional angling action can be found for all species of trout found in Big Blue—and summer Kokanees, especially when they begin their migrating spawn run.

Many anglers know this area as a real fish "funnel" as the downstream currents from the Gunnison River into the Blue Mesa provide a nearly constant food supply. Bait fisherman do well with weighted offerings that are held at or close to the bottom. Trollers who get down to 15-20 foot plus will find browns and rainbow trout near the pylons, and schooling Kokanee salmon in the summer and fall months.

Angling Guide to the

Cebolla Basin

Spanish for the word "onion" Cebolla Basin is a favorite angling area for the deep-water Mackinaw lake trout. Ranging in depths from 40 to well over 125 feet, the Cebolla Basin is home also to large schooling groups of Kokanee salmon. If you're fishing for the Mackinaw, go deep, keep your tube jig with sucker meat at or near the bottom. If you're trolling for Kokanee—3-6 colors of lead core line will keep your lure or spinner at a depth of from 12-25 feet.

C1   **Elk Creek Marina Channel,** Less than 1/2 mile west of the Elk
        Creek Marina
        **N 38o 28.106 to N 38o 27.717 W 107o 11.058 to W
        107o 10.654**

Once you get outside the "no wake" barriers west of the Elk Creek Marina, if you don't have your trolling rods rigged and ready to go, you're missing some golden fishing opportunities. The Elk Creek Channel runs west from the Elk Creek Marina up to the Bay of Chickens and is a prime location for browns and rainbows up close to the "Rocks" we discussed earlier. It is also home to large schools of Kokanee salmon in the main channel area.

Trolling close to the rocks with Rapala floating lures and Count Downs is a great way to pick up on the browns and rainbows. Move out into the deeper waters and use lead-core line or a down-rigger system that will get you down to 16-25 feet deep and you'll start catching Kokanees. Move to the South side rock areas, and find another prime trolling area for rainbows and browns.

C2   **East Elk Creek Camping Area,** Near the "142 mile marker" of
        West Highway 50
        N 38o 28.679 W 107o 10.638

This camping area is designed for large groups that want to camp together. Church groups, Boy/Girl scouts and other large organizations should contact the U.S. Park Service for advance reservations. These are absolutely required. Located approximately 1/2 mile from Highway 50. Fire pits, BB-Qs and restrooms are provided.

C3 **Bay of Chickens Windsurfing/Fishing Area,** Located near the "141 mile marker" on West Highway 50
N 38o 28.689 W 107o 10.836
This daytime camping area is popular with everyone from windsurfers and anglers to picnic campers. Waters in this area are extremely shallow—3-10 feet—and it is one of the few areas on the Blue Mesa Reservoir where water temperatures warm into the upper 60s and lower 70s. Wind surfers "cruise" the shallows on high-tech surf boards equipped with wind sails. Swimmers and waders can enjoy the warmer water temperatures as well, and anglers find some of the deeper waters home to fine trout. Portable toilets are provided. Fall Kokanee snuggers can also find good schooling fish.

C4 **Dry Gulch Campground,** Located at the "140 mile marker" off of West Highway 50.
N 38o 28.867 W 107o 11.276
Dry Gulch has both daytime and overnight campground facilities. It also has a public horse corral open to everyone. Great access back into the National Forest areas for hikers, campers, explorers and photographers. Easy shore fishing access back across Highway 50 to the Blue Mesa Reservoir. Good fishing in a shallow inlet for shore anglers looking for rainbows with bait, spinners and floating Rapala lures.

C5 **Car/Vehicle Pullouts and Turnoffs,** Located between the "140 and 138 mile markers" on Highway 50. There are literally countless access points to the Blue Mesa Reservoir. Many are car/vehicle pullouts and turnoffs located all along the shoreline of the lake. Obviously, they are not named, but they provide great day-camping, picnic and angling access. Some areas provide access to shallow gravel bars where trout have probably never seen a fisherman's lure, jig or bait. Other areas provide anglers the opportunity to fish some of the deeper rock cliffs and drop-offs where large brown trout and fat rainbows lurk.

C6 **Red Creek Campground and Islands,** Highway 50
N 38o 28.610 W 107o 13.709
Daytime and overnight campground facilities, picnic areas, Bar-B-Q's, restrooms, and easy shore fishing access to the Blue Mesa Reservoir.

The Red Creek Campground and road also provides access deep into the Gunnison National Forest, north of the Blue Mesa Reservoir. In the summer, it's ideal for heading into the high country where you'll find miles and miles of streams, creeks and beaver ponds that provide some great brook trout angling opportunities. For the Off-Roader, primitive camper and hiker, trails abound throughout the region.

The Red Creek Islands on the Blue Mesa are prime trout angling spots, with plenty of browns and rainbows available from the shore or in small boats or float tubes. The Red Creek peninsula and the two Islands extend nearly half-way across the Blue Mesa Reservoir. After that, the shallows of yet undeveloped islands and sandbars should be a major warning to Blue Mesa Reservoir boaters. The many warnings about extremely shallow waters should be heeded, and even shallow-draft boats need to exercise extreme caution.

C7   Red Creek Island Shallows
N 38o 27.768 W 107o 13.878

This is an extremely shallow and narrow portion of the Blue Mesa where boaters are urged to SLOW DOWN and look for the warning buoys! Rip though this area into waters that look calm and pristine. . .and you're liable to tear off your propeller and possibly even the bottom of your boat!

When you slow to transit the area, reel in your deep water trolling lines. I guarantee you that downriggers and lead-core lines that are any deeper than 2-3 colors are going to snag on the bottom. However, you may want to stop and throw a jig or lure up on the south side of the buoy line near the large brown rock outcropping. It seems to be home to a combination of rainbows and brown trout that are at the upper end of pan-sized—and good eating!

C8   Cebolla Basin Point, Located at the South/West Cebolla Basin Outlet
N 38o 28.071 W 107o 12.924

Now that you are again angling back to the east in a counter-clockwise direction, near the tip of the small peninsula where the Cebolla Creek area opens up into Cebolla Basin is region that is most often fished by boat anglers. However, if you have a stout 4x4 vehicle and are willing to spend many hours driving the power line roads that cut in from the Lake City Cutoff Road (also known as Sapinero County Road 26) chances are you can drive to this location. **Using a GPS receiver makes it far easier to reach the peninsula.** However boat angling is equally productive.

As you start to turn and go south into the Cebolla Creek arm of the Blue Mesa, the rocks on the southwest shore are home to some excellent lunker brown trout. Rapalas cast towards shore and worked through the shallows back to the boat can bring spectacular results. Trollers stand an equal chance of nailing a trophy fish in and around this honey-hole!

C9   Cebolla Basin Mackinaw "Drift"
N 38o 28.07W 107o 12.924

These are some of the deeper waters found in Cebolla Basin, and some of the most productive for Mackinaw lake trout fishing. Lead-headed Gitzits topped off with sucker meat are the most productive, and best fishing times are when the Blue Mesa is "glass smooth." This usually means very, very early morning angling adventures. Often times by 10 am, the wind has kicked up enough to ruin an even gentle drift-fish through these 50-125 foot waters.

C10   East Waters of Cebolla Basin
38o 28.157 107o 12.073

If you're looking for Mackinaw lake trout, this is one of the early-season areas where the fish are often found in the 20-35 foot waters. Trollers do well with large Flat-fish on down-riggers and lead-core lines. Bait fisherman take lots of fish on Gitzits (lead headed tube jigs) that are topped off with pieces of sucker meat, as well as weighted minnows bounced slowly on the bottom while drift fishing.

C11   Cebolla's Kokanee Troll Area
38o 27.924 107o 12.380

Near the mouth of Cebolla Basin is a prime area to troll for nearly stationary schools of Kokanee salmon. Deeper waters seem to be the best at holding fish in the 16-35 foot depths. Trolling this area, top producers include Dick Nites, Red Arnies, Fox Creek Stingers,

Needlefish and Rapalas. Anglers will find the use of a good quality fish finder to be extremely helpful. Our Hummingbird fish finder model located fish at from 4-6 colors for the lead core line angler, or in the 15-30 foot range for the downrigger.

C12 Cebolla Creek
38o 27.603 107o 12.380

On the south side, down at the mouth of Cebolla Creek is some of the best Mackinaw lake trout fishing that the Blue Mesa has to offer. Most fish are caught in the deeper water depths of from 40-100 feet or more. Trolling with deep-running Flatfish, Mac Attacks and others are favorite lures for this area. If you're down-rigging, or fishing with lead-core line, use your fish finder to locate these lunker lakers that are often holding at or close to the bottom. If you're going to jig for these big fish, make sure that you use enough weight on your lead-headed tube jig or sucker meat offering to allow for drift. Too much weight and you won't feel the fish bite, and too little weight and you'll bounce along the bottom too quickly.

Move up into Cebolla Creek—Spanish for Onion—and you'll find countless rock cliffs, outcroppings, steep drop-offs and even gravel bars that hold the promise of large brown and rainbow trout. Trollers in close to shore will find plenty of action, as will lure and jig anglers.

As you cruise up into the Cebolla Creek Arm of the Blue Mesa Reservoir, be very aware of underwater rocks and trees that provide excellent angling opportunities, but which are also "near the surface" underwater hazards that can be a danger to your boat's propeller. Slow motoring is the key, as well as frequent references to your GPS receiver.

C13 West Side Cebolla Basin Rocks
N 38o 27.587 W 107o 12.380

Fish the west side of Cebolla Basin as it turns into the Cebolla Creek area and you'll want to find the rock formations in this area. They provide plenty of hiding places for brown trout down at the bottom and are a great location for large rainbows. Trollers will find that Rapalas and Rebel lures are great choices, and jig fisherman will want to get in close to the rock outcroppings with Fry Bugs and Maribou jigs topped off with a meal worm or red worm that they can bounce up against the rocks and then work over all the submerged rock areas.

Blue Mesa Reservoir

C14   Underwater Rocks
N 38o 27.477 W 107o 12.121

This is one fishing location where you are again going to be glad that you have a Magellan GPS unit. Once the waters are "summer high" the rocks are fully submerged. However if you follow the coordinates that we've provided, you should be able to find the large rock outcropping that's some 12-18 feet under the water. It provides some great "hiding" areas for big brown trout at the bottom, and just above the rocks, there's almost always a lot of rainbows.

Trollers are going to go home empty handed here, but jig fisherman—casting and vertical jigging—are going to find plenty of fish on Maribous topped with meal worms, and Kastmasters topped with salmon eggs.

C15   Submerged Cliffs
N 38o 27.477 W 107o 12.121

Cruise by this area in your boat and it doesn't look real "trout inviting." However, below the exposed cliffs are a series of rock ledges and drop-offs here in the Cebolla Creek area that we found on our Hummingbird Fish Finder that are ideal for the trout angler that wants to jig for rainbows and browns.

C16   Underwater Trees in the Cebolla Channel
N 38o 27.334 W 107o 12.035

Cebolla has a lot of "underwater structures" that often translate to submerged trees! If you're not careful, they can easily ding a propeller. . .or worse. These trees will be underwater when the waters of the Blue Mesa are high during the summer months, and fully exposed during the spring "low water" times. Vertical jigging in and around this cover can produce a lot of trout at nearly all water level depths. Watch out for the snags from still hidden trees and bushes, but anglers do very well with ultra-light bait and spinner offerings.

C17   Cebolla Creek Boat Camping Area Sign
N 38o 27.278 W 107o 12.025

This area, located on the west side of the Cebolla Creek Arm, has a large sign on the hillside directing boat campers to daytime picnic and overnight camping in the area. There are no facilities at this location, but lots of uncrowded camping sites for the boat angler. If you are looking for seculsion, this is the place.

C18 Rock Cliffs
N 38o 27.224 W 107o 11.888
Move back over to the east side of the Cebolla Creek Arm and you'll find some great rock cliffs that drop off into the water and provide great trout cover from the shore out to depths of 20 plus feet. Look for the browns to be hugging the bank and the rainbows to be in the deeper 12-18 foot waters.

C19 Prominent Rock
N 38o 27.107 W 107o 11.801
Even when the waters rise to normal levels on the Blue Mesa Reservoir, this large and very prominent "boulder" is easy to identify on the western shore of the Cebolla Creek Arm. Don't be surprised to find browns and even rainbows in the area.

C20 Camping Cove
N 38o 27.53 W 107o 11.728
Also located on the West side of the Cebolla Creek Arm and less than 1/4 mile south of Prominent Rock is a cove area that's nearly always occupied. Not only is there easy shore access from the cove to a great camping location, but the cove itself is great for jigging and lure tossing for rainbows and browns.

C21 Mid-Channel Big Pine
N 38o 27.012 W 107o 11.702
Be aware of an under-the-water hazard in this area that may or may not be visible when the Blue Mesa is filled to near capacity. Depending on whether its near or at the surface it can be either a "prop-buster" or a great fishing area. Anchor or drift near this tree, and it's deeper water counterparts and you'll often find a good population of rainbow trout hiding around its bulk and waiting for jigs, sinking small Rapala lures, and even weighted baits.

C22   Trees, Trees and More Trees
N 38o 26.962 up to N 38o 26.894 W 107o 11.539 up to W 107o 11.361

In this area of the main channel in the Cebolla Creek Arm, there are a lot of submerged trees that may or may not be visible in the Blue Mesa. Beware of running over them, but don't overlook the angling possibilities for rainbows which often congregate in and around these underwater obstructions.

C23   Submerged Rock Cliffs
N 38o 26.933 W 107o 11.409

If the water's low, look for these rock cliffs on the east side of the Cebolla Creek Arm. Waters begin to shallow, so look for the fish in 6-12 foot depths. If the waters are high, use your GPS receiver to locate the area and then switch on the fish-finder to locate the big browns that often tuck in on the rock steps.

C24   Twin Trees and Rock Ledges
N 38o 26.810 W 107o 11.192

There are two large pine trees sticking out near the east shore of the Cebolla Creek Arm, visible year-roun. Also, great rock ledges where trout are holding in both shallow and deep waters. Best bet jig and bait anglers is to work the deep waters near the trees. Floating lure anglers with Rapalas and Rebels will do well in the shallows for brown trout.

C25   Single Tree on the Bank
N 38o 26.779 W 107o 11.185

Keep a sharp eye out for this lone tree near the east bank of the Cebolla Creek Arm. When the water levels are up, it provides plenty of cover for rainbows and browns. Thank goodness for your GPS receiver!

C26   Sheer Cliffs and Rock Ledges
N 38o 26.661 W 107o 11.248

Waters this far south in the Cebolla Creek Arm of the Blue Mesa shallow quickly. So that's where you will find the fish that live and feed up in this region. Work the shore lines with jigs for top results on shallow water browns.

C27   Triple Tree Sand Bank
N 38o 26.518 W 107o 11.132

This is one of the last high quality angling areas before the Cebolla Creek Arm literally turns into a creek and the waters become extremely shallow and muddy. Find the three large vertical trees and they will mark a major sandbar and gravel area for you that are ideal for bouncing gently on the bottom a favorite feather jig that's topped off with a meal worm. Keep the retrieve slow and watch the line for even the most gentle tap or bite.

Blue Mesa Reservoir

The Sapinero Basin

Near the west end of Blue Mesa Reservoir lies the Sapinero Basin. For anglers it's not only the gateway to the Lake Fork Arm of the Gunnison on the Blue Mesa Reservoir, but the basin itself holds promise of great shore and boat angling. Shore fisherman do well from the banks for rainbows, browns and the occasional large Mackinaw lake trout, while boat anglers can work easily through large schools of nearly stationary Kokanee salmon, Deep water anglers will find that the bottom of Big Blue in this region is home to some monstrous lake trout.

Just this past spring, Colleen Colborn set a new Blue Mesa Reservoir record when she caught a 36.15 pound Mackinaw by vertical fishing a homemade jig in nearly 80 feet of water near the Sapinero Point area. This area holds a lot of bruisers, and many dedicated anglers believe that a new 40-pound plus Colorado state record lives in the depths of Big Blue.

S1 **The Middle or Dillon Pinnacles Bridge Mackinaw**
"**Drift**" Junction of the Middle Bridge and West Highway 50
N 38º 28.118 W 107º 14.689
Set up an east to west "wind-driven" drift in the deep waters (80-150) feet in this area for big Mackinaws that are lurking near the bottom. Lead-headed tube jigs or Gitzits topped off with a strip of sucker meat hold the promise of large 20 pound plus Lakers.

S2 **The Middle or Dillon Pinnacles Bridge West Kokanee**
"**Drift**" Junction of the Middle Bridge and Highway 50
N 38º 28.108 W 107º 15.251
Set up an east to west wind-driven drift or a very slow troll with spinners on a down rigger or lead-core line in the 3-7 colors range and you'll find a lot of Kokanee salmon.

A good fishfinder can help you locate the schools, and once found you can troll back through them again and again for relatively easy limits.

S3 The North Side of The Middle or Dillon Pinnacles Bridge Turnout/Picnic Area, West Highway 50
N 38o 28.207 W 107o 15.180

From Highway 50, at the Middle or Dillon Pinnacles Bridge, the shore angler will find a convenient parking area, access to plenty of daytime camping areas, picnic tables, rest rooms and access to shore fishing on the Blue Mesa Reservoir. There is a well maintained 2-mile hiking trail that leads back up to the Dillon Pinnacles for a spectacular view of this ancient mud/lava formation. Shore anglers in search of Mackinaw can use the same lead-head tube jig set-up as boat anglers and can easily cast into deep waters. Mackinaw in the 28-30 pound range have been caught by anglers from the bank in this area. Rainbow and brown trout fisherman will find that worms, cheese, crayfish tails and Powerbaits on very light lines in shallow waters (no more than 12 feet deep) seem to produce the most fish for the stringer.

S4 The South Side of the Middle or Dillon Pinnacles Bridge, West Highway 50
N 38o 27.961 W 107o 15.097

If you park on the North side of the Middle Bridge and hike across, or if you access one of the small dirt pullouts, you're likely to find plenty of fishing areas all to yourself. For some reason, few if any shore anglers are ever found on "this" side of the bridge. Shore anglers with salmon eggs, crayfish tails, worms, cheese and Powerbait can regularly take rainbows and browns in the 1-3 pound range. Spinner and spoon anglers also do well, and one lucky angler took a 24-pound lake trout on 6 pound test line with a small gold Kastmaster!

S5 Middle Bridge South-Side Rocks, West Highway 50
N 38o 27.872 W 107o 15.210

If you're a shore angler and have made the effort to hike over to the South Side of the Middle Bridge, expend a little more effort and walk a little to the east of the Bridge where you'll find a secluded cove that rarely gets fished or disturbed by anglers on foot or in a boat. Rock outcroppings are numerous and are home to a lot of 2-pound plus German Brown trout. Maribou feather jigs, Dall-flies and Fry Bugs in green, yellow or black topped off with meal worms and jigged/bounced on the bottom seem to drive these fish wild!

S6   County Road 26 Cutoff from West Highway 50
   N 38o 27.900 W 107o 15.786
This is the dirt road cutoff to Lake City and the Lake Fork Arm of the
Gunnison River. If you want to head out in this direction, it's 16 miles
up the dirt road to Highway 149 and a total of 40 miles to Lake City.
The area is pristine, there's plenty of spectacular views, lots of
"watchable" wildlife and a great place for photography! This is also
where you will find small trails and dirt road cut-offs that will lead you
back down to the Cebolla Basin area if you have a durable 4 x 4
vehicle.

S7   Dillon Pinnacles "Troll"
   N 38o 28.797 W 107o 16.572
This location West of the Middle Bridge is an excellent trolling area,
and a place where you can kick back and take in a spectacular view of
the Dillon Pinnacles while you fish. Keep your lines in the 18-30 feet
depth with downriggers, lead-core line or deep diving lures. Best results
seem to be found on the North side of the Blue Mesa with Rapala
Count Down sinking lures, medium-sized Flat Fish and bright red/gold
or pink/gold spinners.

S8   West Elk Arm "Bluffs" West of the Dillon Pinnacles,
   N 38o 29.564 W 107o 16.939
A lot of drop-offs are found in this area filled with rainbow and brown
trout. Trolling seems to be only marginally successful. Instead, grab the
ultra-light rod and reel and your cast spinners, spoons, Rapalas and
Rebels up close to shore. If the fish are feeding deep, jigging is the best
bet. If the fish are near the surface, try shallow water spinners and
floating lures.

S9   Mouth of the West Elk Creek (Where West Elk Creek flows
   into the Blue Mesa Reservoir)
   N 38o 30.089 W 107o 16.572
Where the West Elk Creek comes into the Blue Mesa is yet another
Boat-In Only camping area that provides plenty of seclusion and little
use by visitors. A designated tent camping area is marked, but there are
no facilities, other than a portable toilet. Fishing in the Blue Mesa for

trout here is marginal only, however if you've got some ultra-light tackle and enjoy a good hike, it's a great place to walk back up the West Elk Creek and fish for brook trout that have likely never seen a spinner or fly.

S10 Peninsula between the West Elk Arm and Soap Creek Arm
N 38o 28.839 W 106o 17.629
Here you have a choice: you can go into deeper waters for schooling Kokanee, rig up for cruising Macs or head into the shallows and troll or jig for rainbows and browns. All are equally productive.

S11 Ponderosa Campground (Mouth of Soap Creek where it flows into the Blue Mesa)
N 38o 31.195 W 107o 17.979
With dirt road access from Highway 92 down by the Blue Mesa Reservoir dam, this campground area is designed for both day-use and overnight camping. Facilities include a small boat ramp, floating dock, restrooms, picnic area and tables, and BB-Q/fire pits.

Angling in the area rates as only fair for shore and boat fishermen on the Blue Mesa. However there is some excellent brook trout fishing to be found in the hiking areas of Soap Creek.

For those wanting to head back into the Gunnison National Forest, the Soap Creek Road continues many miles into the woods to both Commissary and Soap Creek primitive campground areas. A stout pair of hiking shoes, or a four-wheel drive vehicle is highly recommended for this additional exploring.

S12 McIntire Gulch, Soap Creek Road from Highway 92
N 38o 28.567 W 107o 18.655
When the waters of the Blue Mesa Reservoir are low, you can see a good sized peninsula out in front of this day-use camping area which includes picnic tables and restroom facilities. If the water has risen, the peninsula will be submerged, but the fishing for pan-sized rainbows and Kokanee salmon can be very good.

Bait fisherman with traditional salmon eggs, worms, crayfish tails, cheeses and Powerbait seem to have the best success. This area is also a good producer for the shore-fishing Mackinaw angler.

S13)   Blue Mesa Dam Rock Outcroppings
N38º 27.361 W 107º 19.964

If you stand on the dam and follow the north shore some 500 yards away, you will see an area of rock outcroppings and rock steps. These are often loaded with lazy trout. If you are a shore angler, it will be a slow, and sometimes steep, side-hill hike. If you're a boater, it's a 30-second ride from the "strainer" area of the dam.

When the waters are low, look for the fish at 20 feet or greater depths. Once the summer waters rise in the Blue Mesa, a fish finder will show you plenty of trout on just about all of the rock "steps" ranging 10 to 24 feet deep. Best bets for this area are small lead-headed Fry bugs or feathered Maribou jigs topped off with a meal worm. Casting your jigs up to the shoreline and then allowing them to "bounce" along the bottom down the rock steps, can bring about a lot of gentle hits and solid hook-ups!

S14   Blue Mesa Dam "Strainer"
N 38º 27.296 W 107º 20.020

Near the middle of the Blue Mesa Reservoir dam is the water inlet or "strainer" that enables the release of water through the dam into the Morrow Point Reservoir area. The Blue Mesa Reservoir does not have the typical "spillway" found on many other lakes created by dams. The "strainer" is located in some of the deepest waters found anywhere on the lake, and it's a prime area for trolling anglers. Up close to the water inlet area, shallow water trollers find that trout—rainbows and browns—often congregate around the large submerged cement structure at the 8-12 foot levels.

Move back from the inlet structure, and Kokanee salmon fishermen will often find large schools of nearly stationary fish. In the fall months, large concentrations of fish make this popular for deep-water snaggers—night is the most productive time. Shore anglers armed with lanterns, as well as boat anglers equipped with bright lights often report being able to see large schools of spawning salmon throughout the area. With liberal limits of Kokanee salmon available after September 1st, it's a favorite area for the angler and snagger when the salmon move in.

S15 Blue Mesa Dam Highway 92 at the Junction of Highway 50
    N 38o 27.279 W 107o 20.086
At the North side of the Blue Mesa Reservoir dam, there is a small parking area and turnout. Anglers will find plenty of access to shore fishing at the dam area. There are no facilities available but plenty of shore angling opportunities from the rocks of the dam for shallow water browns, and deep water Kokanee salmon.

S16 Lake Fork Campground Shore Fishing Area, Below The RV
    camping sites
    N 38o 27.318 W 107o 19.723
A little-fished area that's within walking distance of all the Lake Fork Campground RV areas and the Marina. Located just off an old "service road," the waters drop off into a host of deep holes that are easily accessible to shore anglers. Boat anglers who want to either anchor or drift through the area and work the 15-20 foot water levels will find some excellent fishing for rainbows, browns and schooling Kokanee salmon. Bait fisherman will find all the traditional favorites are best bets, including meal worms, red worms, nightcrawlers, crayfish tails, salmon eggs, Berkley Power Baits, cheeses and even marshmallows.

S17 Lake Fork Marina Kokanee Troll Area
    N 38o 27.427 W 107o 19.168
Located just outside of the buoys that surround the Lake Fork Marina, this is a prime area for trolling at medium depths for Kokanee salmon schools. Depending upon water conditions and fish finder readings, anglers will often find large schools of salmon in the 12-25 foot range. Lead core line anglers will have best results by trolling 4-5 colors of lead core line. Favorite lures are small Rapalas in gold and orange colors, as well as pink or root beer colored Tasmanian Devils.

S18 Lake Fork Marina, 26 miles to downtown Gunnison. Located
    at the "131 mile marker" on West Highway 50 at the junction of
    Highway 92. 970 641-0348
    N 38o 27.099 W 107o 19.446
Day and overnight camping facilities, shore angling on the Blue Mesa Reservoir, at present, a no-charge public boat ramp, restrooms, showers, National Park Service evening "history" programs for the public,

complete marina facilities with tackle shop, licenses and groceries, small to large boat rentals, slips and fish cleaning area.

NOTE: From the Lake Fork Marina, at the Junction of Highway 50 and Highway 92, you can cross over Highway 92 and it's 41 miles to Crawford, and 52 miles to the Black Canyon National Monument North Rim at Hotchkiss. Or you can stay on Highway 50 and have access through the Pine Creek turn-out to some excellent and uncrowded angling opportunities on the Morrow Point Reservoir. For more information, see the Morrow Point section on page 67.

S19   **Sapinero Bridge,** At West Highway 50 where it crosses the Lake Fork Arm of the Blue Mesa Reservoir
      N 38o 27.133 W 107o 18.481
This is the last bridge found on the Blue Mesa Reservoir as you drive toward Montrose. With several parking pull-outs, it also marks the gateway to the lower part of the Lake Fork Arm of the Gunnison River. Shore fishing can be excellent for German Brown trout working the shallows, as well as big rainbow trout. Work the rock outcroppings and gravel bars on the West side of the bridge for best results.

S20   **Sapinero Island,** Near West Highway 50 and visible from the Town of Sapinero
      N38o 27.410 W 107o 18.235
Depending upon the water level, Sapinero Island can be one acre in size and a great place for lunch, or just a warning pole to alert boaters to shallow water. Still, it seems to be an excellent angling area for Kokanee salmon and an occasional lunker lake trout. Trolling in and around the exposed or submerged island with Rapalas, Dick Nites, Needlefish and Fox Creek lures can put a lot of Kokanee in the creel. Keep your lines shallow (6-15 feet).

S21   **Mac Point**
      N 38o 27.610 W 107o 18.449
This is a legendary area to which Mackinaw lake trout anglers flock as there seems to be a lot of baitfish and Kokanee salmon in the area that keep some real "monster" laker-lunkers well fed. Boat anglers trolling

large Flat Fish lures, Rapalas and jointed-Rebels continue to report excellent success on the big fish. However, if the Macs aren't cooperating, small Rapalas, Needlefish, Red Arnies, and Tasmanian Devils can boat a lot of Kokanee salmon in this area.

S22   The Town of Sapinero, Highway 50
N 38o 27.466 W 107o 18.186

A small turn-out with a gas station and grocery store that is sometimes occupied and sometimes not. For the angler, this area is known for "Mac Point" where a shallow shore stretches out into the Blue Mesa Reservoir, and is often home to large Mackinaw lake trout that continually top the scales at 25 pounds or more.

Blue Mesa Reservoir

Morrow Point Reservoir

Although this is not "part" of the Blue Mesa Reservoir, it is part of the system and the fishing opportunities are just too good not to describe.

S23   **Pine Creek Trail**, 130 Mile Marker off Highway 50, Access to Morrow Point Reservoir
      N 38o 26.774 W 107 20.521

The Pine Creek turnoff from Highway 50 provides access to the often under-fished and un-fished Morrow Point Reservoir. If you're towing a trailer, make sure that you park the trailer in the "upper" parking area. From there, it's a 3/4 mile drive down to the "top" of the trailhead and final parking area. Restrooms, picnic tables and BB-Qs have been placed in the day campground area. To access the fishing area, hike 20 minutes downhill (233 steps) to the bottom of the Black Canyon. This is an area where the fish are large and they rarely see an angler.

For the hiker and hiking angler, at the bottom of the Black Canyon is a 3/4 mile trail that was once the narrow gauge railroad bed that ran from Cimarron to Crested Butte. The trail runs alongside some fine fishing waters in this upper part of the Morrow Point Reservoir. These waters range from placid and nearly calm to roaring torrents. Early in the morning, the waters are often calm and the pools are deep. However, as water is released from the Blue Mesa Reservoir, the water levels rise and so does the flow rate!

In the spring and summer, the area enjoys great spincast and fly fishing from shore for hungry trout. In the late fall, the area is famous for it's land-locked Kokanee salmon run, and anglers say that Mepps Gold and red/white spinners, as well as large red or orange streamer flies are top salmon catchers. During late August all the way to early October, the salmon are often found in large numbers at and near the base of the Pine Creek Trail area.

For angling on the many other isolated waters found throughout the Morrow Point Reservoir area, contact Elk Creek Marina (970 641-0707) for guided angling trips throughout the summer and fall. Believe me, here is a large reservoir loaded with rainbows, browns, brookies, green river cutthroats, Kokanee salmon and Mackinaws!

Angling Guide to the

Lake Fork Arm Of The Blue Mesa Reservoir.

Because of the huge expanse of the Blue Mesa Reservoir, many anglers, boaters, campers and lake users consider the Lake Fork Arm of the Gunnison to be a separate recreation area. Unless you are an avid hiker and do not mind trekking many miles from even the remote roads, the Lake Fork belongs the boat-owning angler, camper, photographer and explorer.

With access to a boat—be it a small motorized fishing skiff or luxury pontoon craft—rarely will you see any shore anglers on the Lake Fork Arm. While there are hundreds of great shore fishing opportunities, the vast majority of boat fisherman find they can catch plenty of fish without ever setting foot on shore.

LA1 **Sapinero Bridge Pylons Sapinero Bridge** over West Highway 50
N 38o 27.083 W 107o 18.442

Since fishing directly from the Sapinero Bridge is prohibited, angling in and around the pillars is a "boat access" proposition only. Casting small Rapala and Rebel lures near these pillars can produce a lot of pan-fish trout. Floater lures will attract fish in the shallow water depths at the 4-8 foot levels. Sinking lures are best worked in the 10-15 foot water depths.

Trolling between the 3rd, 4th, and 5th pylons with lead-core line at a depth of from 12-18 feet (3-4 colors) with Fox Creek lures and other spinners is a great way to find stationary schools of Kokanee salmon. If you get a hit and land a fish, troll back through the same area at the same depth and you'll often find a lot more hungry salmon eager to take your spinner.

LA2 **Sapinero Cove,** South of West Highway 50 at the Sapinero Bridge, and below the new houses in the Sapinero/Lake Fork Area
N 38o 26.914 W 107o 18.475

This small cove is located just below all of the houses seen on the south of the Sapinero Bridge and can be accessed by both shore and boat anglers. Shore fishermen will find the cove loaded with shore rocks and drop-offs are ideal for bait fishing. Rock steps run from 6-25 foot depths and rainbows and browns are in the shallow waters early in the season. They usually move to the deeper and cooler depths later in the summer months. Boat anglers who jig up close to the shore and allow their jigs to "float" down, are top producers. Maribou feather jigs, Fry Bugs, and small Rapalas are the best bets.

LA3 Sapinero Bridge Rocks South/East Side of the Sapinero Bridge of West Highway 50
N 38o 27.003 W 107o 18.367
Park on the west side of the Sapinero Bridge along Highway 50 and hike back across. On the south are often overlooked fishing areas. The nearly—and often—submerged island at the southeast corner of the Sapinero bridge is home to a lot of shallow water brown trout that are rarely tempted by lure or jig. Boat anglers have the advantage in being able to fish the back side of the submerged island and shallows—watch for the "boat warning" stands. Work the areas around the island with shallow diving lures and spinners.

LA4 First Lake Fork Arm "Rocks"
N 38o 26.815 W 107o 17.843
As you boat up into the Lake Fork Arm southeast from the Sapinero Bridge, the first set of "rock cliffs" are on the north side of the Lake Fork and within sight of the Bridge. Jigging in close to the rocks and casting small lures are usually most productive for the browns and rainbows that lurk near the rock cliffs. If the fishing is slow, look to the south side of the Lake Fork Arm and you'll find a small cove that's worth a slow troll.

LA5 First Lake Fork Arm "Cove"
N 38o 26.379 W 107o 17.309
This small cove on the south side of the Lake Fork Arm is significant because it's so easily accessible by anglers and provides some great brown and rainbow fishing. Jigs, spinners and lures work equally well. Look across the lake Fork Arm to the north side and you'll see "rocks" that are worth fishing as well. In the meantime, hook up a trolling rod and pick up some of the schooling Kokanee that often work through the area.

LA6 Lake Fork's Black Rocks and Deadfall 3/4 miles up the Lake Fork from the Sapinero Bridge
N 38o 26.606 W 107o 17.100

Less than 3/4 mile up the north east shore of the Lake Fork Arm is an area easily recognized because of its distinct black rocks and numerous deadfall trees that litter the high shoreline. While it may not look like much in terms of scenery, it's a great fishing area for browns, rainbows and even an occasional brook trout.

LA7 Pine Point Approximately 1-mile up from the Sapinero Bridge on the Lake Fork Arm.
N 38o 26.135 W 107o 16.569

This prominent point on the North Side of the Lake Fork Arm is located about 1-mile from the Sapinero Bridge and is easily identified by a large stand of pine trees that reach close to the water. A host of rock outcroppings make this area great for anglers. Get in close to shore for the best angling, but beware of snags among the rocks. Vertical jigging with Maribou jigs and Fox Creek or Mepps Spinners are top producers in this area.

LA8 Dead Pine Cove Near The Lake Fork Arm Boat Camping Area
N 38o 25.913 W 107o 16.574

There are several large vertical dead pine trees that help mark this cove, also several excellent rock outcroppings and rock steps, as well as great shore access for the boater. The Lake Fork Arm Camping area is nearby and was designed for boating campers—a great spot to "pull-out" and put ashore for daytime and overnight camping. There are no facilities, but a marked trail and the designated camping areas are easy to find. For those that want to get away from it all on their angling vacation, the Lake Fork Arm camping area is but one of four true boat-camping areas that are provided by the National Park Service on the Blue Mesa Reservoir.

LA9 Rock Outcroppings 1.5 miles up the Lake Fork Arm
N 38o 25.768 W 107o 16.360

Large rock outcroppings are located on the east side of the Lake Fork Arm about 1.5 miles up from the Sapinero Bridge. It's an excellent trout angling area where the drop offs are steep, the cuts are easy to find and fish, and lots of browns and rainbows congregate in waters that range from 4 to 15 feet.

LA10   Eagle's Nest Rocks
N 38o 25.698 W 107o 16.304

This steep rock cliff rises nearly 125 feet straight up on the east shore of the Lake Fork Arm of the Blue Mesa. Near the top is a large eagle's nest. Nobody in recent time has seen any nesting eagles in it, but it makes an easy way to identify the area. The water's below have some excellent trout angling for the jig fisherman.

LA11   Steep Wall Cove
N 38o 25.420 W 107o 15.631

Located on the east side of the Lake Fork Arm, the cove has steep walls and good bank cuts and outlets where the trout are often lying in the shallow waters up close to shore. Slow your speed and watch for the "Shallow Water Marker Warning" post in the middle of the channel to avoid a "bent prop." Heed the warnings!

LA12   Powerline Waterfall
N 38o 25.232 W 107o 15.525

High overhead powerlines cross east to west above the Lake Fork Arm here. Watch for a steep creek and waterfall. It's a wonderful area for photographers as well as great place to find "lazy" trout in the deeper waters hoping the current will carry an easy meal to them! Jigs topped with meal worms and red worms bounced along the bottom are best bets, as are small bright spinners such as the Fox Creek Stinger.

LA13   Rock Narrows and Shallow Cove
N 38o 24.237 W 107o 14.914

One of the last fishing areas before reaching the "log jam" below the Gateway Campground Area. Good trout fishing in the spring and summer months, and plenty of Kokanee salmon congregate here in the late fall. It's a favorite boat angling spot for fly fisherman, spincast anglers and snaggers when the salmon start their yearly migratory spawning run.

LA14   Log Jam

A large log jam area below the Gateway Campground on the Lake Fork Arm of the Gunnison on the Blue Mesa Reservoir. This area provides fair to good trout fishing in the late spring and summer months for the boat and shore angler. Best bets are shallow water trolling using Rapala and Rebel lures, Tasmanian Devils and casting bright spinners from boat and shore. For the shore angler, the "Log Jam" can be easily reached by walking about 1/4 mile north from the Gateview Campground area.

In the fall, the Log Jam serves as a major fish trap for spawning Kokanee salmon that are trying to make their way back upstream into the river sections of the Lake Fork Arm. Keep in mind that each year over 100,000 Kokanee salmon are released into the river portion of the Lake Fork Arm of the Gunnison. Obviously, they all aren't going to spawn, but the numbers are significant enough to attract both river and lake anglers starting in early September and lasting as long as the spawning run continues. The run usually provides good angling from late August to mid-October of each year.

Anglers will find that Kokanee become extremely aggressive during the spawning months and strike lures, jigs and flies passed in front of them. Bright and flashy lures, as well as large bright and gaudy flies are top producers.

After September 1st, snagging for Kokanee salmon is legal on the Blue Mesa Reservoir, including all areas of the Lake Fork Arm. Favorites for snaggers are large weighted treble hooks cast out, allowed to sink to the bottom and then pulled back rapidly in hopes of "hooking into" a fish in the spawning school. Snagging is controversial and the Colorado Wildlife Commission is seriously considering prohibiting the process in the future. Check the regulations for current rulings.

Blue Mesa Reservoir

Shopping and Dining In Gunnison

The town of Gunnison divides easily along a north-south, east-west axis defined by U.S. Highway 50 (east and west) and Colorado Highway 135 (north). Listed below are general locations and within them, specific retail and dining establishments to make your stay in the area even more pleasant. They are located both by street address, with telephone number, and by GPS coordinates.

GPS Check
Downtown Gunnison. Main Street (Highway 135) at Tomichi Blvd(Highway 50)
N 38 º 32.666 W 106 º 55.611
The center of town with plenty of great restaurants and a unique opportunity to unwind from the hassles of big city life.

North Main Street—Also known as Highway 135 North

1N **Shady Island RV Resort,** 2714 Highway 135 (1 1/4 miles north of Wal-Mart Gunnison, CO 81230 970 641-0416
N 38º 35.025 W 106º 55.306
A small resort with cabins and full recreational vehicle hookups—day, week and seasonal rates available. Member of the Colorado Association of Campgrounds, Cabins and Lodges.

2N **Garlic Mikes Restaurant,** 2674 Highway 135 (1 mile north of Wal-Mart) Gunnison, CO 81230 970 641-2493
N 38º 35.973 W 106º 55.276
Garlic Mikes is one of the newest restaurants in the GRT and specializes in some of the finest Italian food found anywhere. Specialties include pasta, veal, poultry, beef and seafood. Open for Lunch and Dinner.

Angling Guide to the

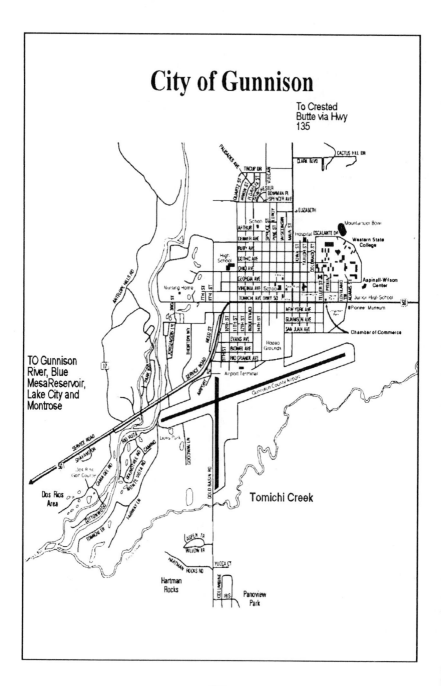

City of Gunnison

To Crested Butte via Hwy 135

TO Gunnison River, Blue Mesa Reservoir, Lake City and Montrose

Dos Rios Area

Tomichi Creek

Hartman Rocks

Panoview Park

3N   **Tall Texan Campground**, 2460 Highway 135 (3/4 mile north of Wal-Mart) at County Rd 11 Gunnison, CO 81230 970 641-2927
     N 38o 34.811 W 106o 55.177
With 110 shady RV sites, the Tall Texan Campground offers daily, weekly, monthly and seasonal rates. Facilities include playground area, cable TV and coin-operated Laundromat. Member Colorado Association of Campgrounds, Cabins & Lodges.

4N   **Wal-Mart**, 900 N. Main Street (Highway 135) Gunnison, CO 81230 970-641-1733
     N 38o 33.267 W 106o 55.590
Located at the extreme North end of Main street (Highway 135), Wal Mart has a large stock of fishing and camping gear at discount prices. Artificial baits, lures, flies, line, rods/reels, tents and sleeping bags. Also, just about anything else that you will need while away from home.

5N   **Van's Food Store**, 905 N. Main Street (Highway 135) Gunnison, CO 81230 970-641-4729
     N 38o 33.250 W 106o 55.616
Van's Food Store is located at the upper end of Main Street, or Highway 135, and is a great place for the summer camper and angler to make their "last" stop before heading north towards Crested Butte and some of the fine alpine lake and river fishing found in the high mountain country. They have gasoline for vehicles and plenty of food, package goods, ice and beer for the individual.

6N   **Cafe Silvestre**, Home Made Mexican Food 903 N. Main Street (Highway 135) Gunnison, CO 81230 970-641-4001
     N 38o 33.221 W 106o 55.614
Cafe Silvestre is wedged in between High Mountain Liquor and Vans Food Store. This means you can pick up your favorite beverages, grab some great Mexican food and then top off your gas tank—all in one stop! Cafe Silvestre has both dine-in and take-out facilities, and all of their food is made-to-order. The prices are reasonable, the portions are generous and the food is excellent. Highly recommended!

7N **High Mountain Liquor,** 901 N. Main Street Gunnison, CO
81230 970-641-6304
N 38º 33.204 W 106º 55.609

High Mountain Liquor is a favorite "stop-off" point for travelers
heading to Crested Butte and the many other popular fishing and
camping areas located in the Gunnison River Territory. The store has
a complete stock of beers, wines, liquors and spirits.

8N **Coast To Coast,** 821 North Main Street (Highway 135)
Gunnison, CO 81230 970-641-2616
N 38º 33.136 W 106º 55.632

Having recently moved into their "high visibility" new location, Coast
To Coast is now a complete hardware store with a host of picnic and
camping items, licenses, etc.

9N **Duncan 4x4 Repair and Automotive Service,** 811 N. Main
Street (Highway 135) Gunnison, CO 81230 970-641-4444
N 38º 33.148 W 106º 55.640

Duncan 4x4 Repair and Automotive Service are the folks who can
repair just about anything with wheels. If your car, truck, van, camper
or recreational vehicle fails when on your summer camping or fishing
trip, they can supply you with everything from a new tire to a new
transmission quickly and get you back on or off the road to continue
your travels.

10N **Palisades Restaurant and Saloon,** 820 N. Main Street
(Highway 135) Gunnison, CO 81230 970-641-9223
N 38º 33.163 W 106º 55.558

The Palisades Restaurant and Saloon is located near the North end of
Main Street and is full-service restaurant and bar. Open for lunch and
dinner, their menu specializes in everything from steaks to burgers, as
well as a host of Cajun specialties and adult drinks—wine, beer, liquors
and spirits.

11N **Hi-Country Service,** 700 N. Main Street (Highway 135)
Gunnison, CO 81230 970-641-3894
N 38º 33.094 W 106º 55.590

A complete food and Phillips 66 gas service convenience station and convenience store, along with full self-service laundry facilities. You can gas your car, eat your fill and wash the dust and dirt from your vacation clothes, all at the same time.

12N   **Timberline Jeep/Motorcycle/Bike Rentals,** 701 N. Main Street (Highway 135) Gunnison, CO 81230 970-641-4335 **N 38o 33.113 W 106o 55.572**

Timberline Jeep/Motorcycle/Bike Rentals is located at the last stop light leaving Gunnison north towards Crested Butte at Highway 135 and Denver Avenue. They offer 4x4 vehicles, motorcycles and bicycles for day, week and even hourly use.

13N   **Wilson Realty,** 100 E. Gothic Ave (Corner of Gothic and Main Street) Gunnison, CO 81230 970 641-2169 **N 38o 32.933 W 106o 55.597**

A valley leader in ranches and acreage sales, Wilson Realty has an extensive free Summer Guide to Recreational Property in and around the Gunnison area.

14N   **Prudential/Becky Hamlin Realty,** 411 N. Main Street, Gunnison, CO 970 641-6691 **N 38o 33.284 W 106o 55.592**

A full service realty offering listings that include city or country homes, homesite, ranches, recreational acreage, business or commercial properties. Call for all your rental needs as well.

15N   **Monarch Realty,** 400 N. Main Street Gunnison, CO 81230 970 641-1900 **N 38o 32.874 W 106o 55.593**

Monarch Realty is a full-service, all broker real estate office with listings for ranches, acreage, recreational properties and many "vacation" home offerings.

16N   **Dennis Steckel Realtors,** 401 N. Main Street Gunnison, CO 81230 970 641-2235 **N 38o 32.869 W 106o 55.617**

Dennis Steckel Realtors lists and sells a lot of ranch properties and vacation homes in the Gunnison River Territory.

17N   **Farrells' Restaurant,** 310 N. Main Street (Highway 135) Gunnison, CO 81230 970-641-2655
      N 38o 32.833 W 106o 55.595

Farrells' opened in 1990 and has established a great reputation for super lunches, patio dining and spectacular fresh breads, pies, pastries and homemade soup.

18N   **Hi-Kountry Kitchen-Bakery,** 302 N. Main Street (Highway 135) Gunnison, CO 81230 970-641-1489
      N 38o 32.833 W 106o 55.595

Fresh baked pastries and donuts are the best way to start any morning. Their apple fritters are exceptional, the coffee mugs deep and their "sack lunches" ideal if you are planning to spend a day on the Blue Mesa Reservoir.

19N   **Gunnison Camera Center,** 241 N. Main Street (Highway 135) Gunnison, CO 81230 970-641-1193
      N 38o 32.828 W 106o 55.599

Gunnison Camera Center is the most complete film and camera store in the region. With a complete line of film for all outdoorsman's needs, they specialize in processing your print or slide film "fast." Clip their ad in the at the back of this book for a 10% savings offer on all film processing. They can also provide camera repair, conventional and single-use cameras for all your photo needs.

20N   **UniGlobe Mountain Travel** 234 N. Main Street, Suite 2C (Highway 135) Gunnison, CO 81230 970-641-3460
      N 38o 32.785 W 106o 55.581

A full service travel agency for locals or returning sportsmen and sportswomen looking for discounts on air travel, hotel and car rentals. Call Toll Free at 1-800 641-6770.

21N   **Chatterbox Deli,** 206 N Main Street (Highway 135) Gunnison, CO 81230 970 641-0330
      N 38o 32.154 W 106o 55.589

A local deli and sandwich shop that's famous for great sandwiches and home-made teas. Ideal place to stop for lunch or an early dinner. Or take along their a large "sack lunches" while out fishing for the day.

22N   **The TuneUp Bike/Rock Climbing Shop,** 222 N. Main Street (Highway 135), Gunnison CO 81230 970 641-0285
       N 38º 32.655 W 106º 55.579

A full-service bike shop, rock-climbing and ski shop that has summer bike rentals, full service and parts for any bikes in need of repair. Fast and dependable, the TuneUp also has a full line of books, magazines, maps, bike apparel and some great rock climbing gear.

23N   **Gunnison Vitamin & Health Food Store,** 213 N. Main Street (Highway 135), Gunnison, CO 81230
       N 38º 32.839 W 106º 55.542

If you are conscious about what you eat, Gunnison Vitamin & Health Food Store has a complete line of healthy organic foods, vitamins, supplements, produce and over 132 herbs and spices. They also make "Gunnison Solution," hand and body cream, a special blend of skin healing ingredients in ointment form that should be in every angler's and camper's gear box. Stop in for a free sample. The results are best "felt" to be believed.

24N   **Bookworm Book Store,** 211 N. Main Street (Highway 135) Gunnison, CO 81230 970-641-3693
       N 38º 32.828 W 106º 55.559

The Bookworm is a full-line book store serving the avid reader and the dedicated sportsman with a full line of books on Colorado's great outdoors and maps for campers and anglers to all of the Gunnison River Territory.

25N   **Oasis Cafe and Bar,** 142 N. Main Street Gunnison, CO 81230 303) 641-0647
       N 38º 32.738 W 106º 55.567

A favorite local watering hole where everyone—ranchers, cowboys, college professors, tourists, campers and visiting anglers—come to unwind, swap tales and enjoy good drinks and company.

Angling Guide to the

26N   **German Brown Flies & Tackle**, 134 North Main Street
(Highway 135) Gunnison, CO 81230 970 641-5370
N 38o 32.739 W 106o 55.544

A full-service fly fishing shop designed for novice fly fisherman or the experienced angler. Complete line of rods, reels, waders, belly-boats, line, clothing, accessories, maps, sporting books, fly tying materials and lots and lots of the most popular flies for fishing in the Gunnison River Territory. At last count, they have over 17,000 of the most popular flies in stock.

27N   **Steaming Bean Coffee Company**, 120 N. Main Street
(Highway 135) Gunnison, CO 81230 970 641-2408
N 38o 32.751 W 106o 55.618

Open at 7 am, they serve a wide variety of great coffees, everything from regular to gourmet blends, to help get your day started.

28N   **W Cafe**, 114 N. Main Street (Highway 135) Gunnison, CO
81230 970 641-1744
N 38o 32.686 W 106o 55.631

Open early, early for the visiting sportsmen or the local cattle rancher. The W Cafe has large portions, reasonable prices and a truly bottomless cup of coffee.

29N   **Cottonwoods**, 111 N. Main Street (Highway 135)
Gunnison, Co 81230 970 641-4728
N 38o 32.685 W 106o 55.614

One of Gunnison's nicest gift stores with a complete line of sporting and fashion clothing, footwear, global positioning system receivers, gift items designed for the sportsmen and sportswomen, and a super coffee bar! Here the coffee is always hot, the specialty blends are spectacular and the gift items second to none! Complete line of Sea Kayaks and accessories. Also, stop in to rent, buy or just to learn about the Global Positioning System from this licensed Magellan dealer.

East Tomichi Ave, also known as East Highway 50.

1E   **Gunnison Pioneer Museum** 801 E. Tomichi Ave. (East Highway 50) Corner of South Adams and Tomichi Ave. Gunnison, CO 81230 970-641-4530
  N 38o 32.650 W 106o 55.057

The Gunnison Pioneer Museum is located at the East end of Gunnison and is a great way to learn about the history of the Gunnison River Territory. Exhibits begin when the dinosaurs walked the area, tell how the Ute Indians were displaced by arriving miners and ranchers, and how the City of Gunnison has grown—and continued to grow. With several acres of open displays and a lot of enclosed museum areas, it's a great way to spend a morning or afternoon with the family and learn more about this historically rich area.

2E   **McDonald's Restaurant**, 800 E. Tomichi Ave. (East Highway 50) Corner of North Adams and Tomichi Ave. Gunnison, CO 81230 970-641-5050
  N 38o 32.680 W 106o 55.071

McDonald's and it's Golden Arches is located just across from the Gunnison Pioneer Museum. Recently expanded, they now feature the full service Mac-Menu for breakfast, lunch and dinner fare. Drive through service is available for you summer campers and anglers.

3E   **Gunnison River Territory Visitor, Center Chamber of Commerce**, 500 E. Tomichi Ave. (East Highway 50) Gunnison, CO 81230 970 641-1501
  N 38o 32.681 W 106o 55.270

The Gunnison River Territory Visitor Center has been recently remodeled and greatly expanded. For the visiting recreationist, it's a MUST STOP! They can provide the angler, camper, photographer, off-roader and hiker with the latest maps, brochures and literature concerning where-to-stay, where-to-eat, and where-to- travel information.

Angling Guide to the

4E   **Jorgenson Recreation Complex/Park**, 501 E. Tomichi Ave
(East Highway 50) Gunnison, CO 81230
N 38o 32.651 W 106o 55.238

Jorgenson Park not only provides some great daytime picnic and family
play areas, but it also sports a "kids only" fishing pond that is well
stocked with rainbow trout for the young angler. No charge for fishing,
no license required for the little fisherman or fisherwomen, and just
about any of the popular baits—salmon eggs, cheeses, Berkley Power
baits and worms work well.

During the summer months, various programs for children
provide both entertainment and education. The city, chamber of
commerce and various groups work hard to make the Complex safe and
fun.

5E   **Quarter Circle Restaurant**, 323 E. Tomichi Ave. (East Highway
50) Gunnison, CO 81230 970 641-0542
N 38o 32.656 W 106o 55.408

The Quarter Circle Restaurant remains a true Gunnison River Territory
institution. The food is very good, the prices are extremely reasonable
and the portions are generous. The specialty is BB-Q beef ribs and
they're excellent.

6E   **Daylight Donuts**, 315 E. Tomichi Ave. (East Highway 50)
Gunnison, CO 81230 970 641-1163
N 38o 32.655 W 106o 55.426

Daylight Donuts specializes in fresh baked donuts and pastries for the
early-riser. Everything is fresh-baked daily—most all the donuts are
gone by early morning, so don't wait!

7E   **Blue Iguana Mexican Food**, 303 E. Tomichi Ave. (East
Highway 50) Gunnison, CO 81230 970 641-3403
N 38o 32.654 W 106o 55.437

The Blue Iguana boasts fine home cooked Mexican food, and is open
for lunch and dinner. Take-out is available, and their "smothered
burritos" and "chimichungas" are worth a summer stop. Beer and wine
are available.

8E   **Tenderfoot River Rafting and Outdoors**, 300 E. Tomichi Gunnison, CO 81230 970 641-2200 (800) Raft-W-Us
N 38º 32.654 W 106º 55.397

Tenderfoot River Rafting has a host of "river running" experiences to suit the needs of everyone from the angler to the river rafting thrill seeker. Daily fishing trips down the upper/lower Gunnison, Arkansas River and into the Black Canyon.

9E   **Amoco Gas Station and Convenience Store/High Mountain Tackle, Fly Shop and Guide Service**, 211 E. Tomichi Ave. (East Highway 50) Gunnison, CO 81230 970-641-4243
N 38º 32.664 W 106º 55.492

The Amoco Gas Station and Convenience Store is a complete service visitor stop. Gasoline, groceries and an enclosed car wash are available. Sharing the facilities is High Mountain Tackle catering to the "most serious" fly angler.

10E   **Conoco Gasoline/Car Wash and Convenience Store**, 201 E. Tomichi Ave. (East Highway 50) Gunnison, CO 81230 970-641-3536
N 38º 32.657 W 106 55.512

One of Gunnison's most modern 24-hour gasoline and convenience stores complete with a drive-in brushless car/vehicle wash. Grab a bunch a goodies and snacks, a tank load of gas and a car wash.

11E   **I-Bar Ranch**, 1-mile East of Gunnison on Highway 49 from Highway 50 Gunnison, CO 81230 970 641-4100
N 38º 32.460 W 106º 54.065

The I-Bar Ranch is a summer evening theater whose motto is "It's where the West Was Fun!" An elaborate western music show that's ideal evening entertainment for the entire family! Nightly throughout the entire summer!

12E   **Wet Grocer**, 202 E. Tomichi Ave. (East Highway 50) Gunnison, CO 81230 970 641-5054
W 38º 32.679 N 106º 55.494

A full service beer, wine and spirits store.

Angling Guide to the

13E **Gunnison Sporting Goods,** 133 East Tomichi Ave. (East
Highway 50) Gunnison, CO 81230 970-641-5022
N 38º 32.655 W 106º 55.576
Gunnison Sporting Goods is a favorite spot for anglers, summer
campers and hunters to load up on gear, bait and the latest "hotspot
fishing information." Global Positioning System receivers for sale.
Family owned and operated since 1990, they pride themselves in
providing all outdoorsmen and women with plenty of personal help and
assistance.

14E **Total Gas and Convenience Store,** 134 E. Tomichi Ave. (East
Highway 50) Gunnison, CO 81230
N 38º 32.652 W 106º 55.551
A 24-hour gas and convenience store with a host of auto/marine oils
and supplies for every sportsman or sportswoman's needs.

West Tomichi Ave, also known as West Highway 50.

1W **Sidewalk** Cafe, 113 W. Tomichi Ave (West Highway 50)
Gunnison, CO 81230   970 641-4130
N 38 º 32.699 W 106 º 55.655
The Sidewalk Cafe's motto is "home of the biggest pancake." Obviously
it's a popular choice for early morning anglers in search of "plenty" of
breakfast eats!

2W **Manning-Manning Realtors,** 123 W. Tomichi Ave. (West
Highway 50) Gunnison, CO 81230 970 641-2040
N 38º 32.694 W 106º 55.660
Long established realtor who specializes in ranch properties that are
ideal for raising cattle or for just plain enjoying large areas of the great
outdoors.

3W **Timbers Sports Bar and Grille,** 136 W. Tomichi Ave. (West
Highway 50) Gunnison, CO 81230   970 641-1491
N 38 º 32.681 W 106 55.668
Timbers Sports Bar is a favorite "watering hole" for locals and
sportsmen that features a complete "sport" motif. With a host of

satellite TV sport programs constantly being aired, the true sport fan is "never out of touch."

4W **Subway Sandwich Shop,** 136 W. Tomichi Ave. (West Highway 50) Gunnison, CO 81230 970 641-1853
    N 38 o 32.680 W 106 o 55.670
The Subway Sandwich Shop can provide nearly any submarine-type sandwich you want. Dine-in or take-out is available, and for anglers with a.1 appetite, Subway can provide some of the biggest sandwiches you can hope to consume!

5W **Gene Taylors Sporting Goods,** 201 West Tomichi Ave. (West Highway 50) Corner of Wisconsin and Tomichi Ave. Gunnison, CO 81230 (970-641-1845)
    N 38 o 32.642 W 106 o 55.671
Without question, Gene Taylor's Sporting Goods is the most fully equipped outdoor's person retail store in Gunnison. They carry a most complete line of fishing tackle and outdoor recreation/camping equipment. Rods, reels, waders, flies, lures, baits, and accessories are available. Global Positioning System receivers are available for rent or sale.

6W **Mario's Pizzeria Home of Great Italian Food,** 213 West Tomichi Ave. (West Highway 50) Gunnison, CO 81230 970 641-1374
    N 38 o 32.644 W 106 o 55.678
Mario's Pizzeria is a lot more than great pizzas. They feature a full service menu with homemade spaghetti, calzones, sandwiches and beer.

7W **John Roberts Motor Works,** 231 W. Tomichi Ave. (West Highway 50) Gunnison, CO 81230 970 641-0920
    N 38o 32.633 W 106o 55.715
Gunnison's only authorized General Motors, Chevrolet, Buick, Oldsmobile, Pontiac and Geo dealer and repair station. They welcome repair service on any and all makes of cars, trucks and vans. And they are great at getting summer visitors with vehicle problems back on the road again quickly.

Angling Guide to the

8W **The Cattlemen Inn and Restaurant,** 301 West Tomichi (West Highway 50) Located at Pine and Tomichi Ave. Gunnison, CO 81230 970 641-1061
N 38 o 32.654 W 106 o 55.787

The Cattlemen Inn has been around for over 50 years and has continued to serve the lodging and restaurant needs of the Gunnison area all that time. Featuring low-cost comfortable lodging, the Inn has two restaurants, a bar and lounge. They serve breakfast, lunch and dinner daily, and often feature "all you can eat" beef rib specials!

9W **Safeway Market,** 112 South Spruce, Corner of Spruce and Tomichi Ave. (West Highway 50) Gunnison, CO 81230   970 641-0787)
N 38 o 32.612 W 106 o 55.830

The Safeway Market store is located most conveniently on Highway 50 and can provide the summer angler or camper with all grocery needs. They also have a full-service deli with sliced meats and cheeses, sack lunches and prepared dishes.

10W House of China, 405 West Tomichi Ave. (West Highway 50) Gunnison, CO 81230 970 641-0667
N 38 o 32.669 W 106 o 55.886

The House of China is open for lunch and dinner and provides excellent Szechuan, Cantonese and Mandarin cuisine. Full-service bar and restaurant, as well as take-out orders seven-days a week.

11W City Market, 400 W. Virginia Ave. Located at the corner of Spruce and Virginia Avenue Gunnison, CO 81230   970 641-3816
N 38 o 32.763 W 106 o 55.826

The City Market is Gunnison's other full-service grocery store that keeps long-hours for visiting recreationists. The market also features a complete bakery for a host of fresh-baked goods that include pastries, bagels, bread, cookies and much more.

12W Mi Casita Restaurant Mexican Food, 515 West Tomichi Ave. (West Highway 50) Gunnison, CO 81230 970 641-5106
N 38 o 32.661 W 106 o 55.972

Mi Casita's features both dine-in and take-out homemade Mexican food for lunch and dinner. If you've got a big appetite—try their selection of "big burritos" complete with homemade salsa.

13W Berfield's Stage Stop, 519 West Tomichi Ave. (West Highway 50) Gunnison, CO 81230 970 641-5782
N 38 o 32.660 W 106 o 55.995
Berfield's provides a full convenience store, sporting goods, gasoline and ice. Stop off with a big fish and let Randy take your picture to add to his collection of lunker fish and lucky anglers!

14W Trader's Rendezvous, 516 W. Tomichi Ave. (West Highway 50) Gunnison, CO 81230 970 641-5077
N 38o 32.680 W 106o 55.997
This is a "must stop" location for all visiting sportsmen. Trader's Rendezvous not only has licenses, it also is home to the largest collection of mounted trophies and horns anywhere in the Rocky Mountains, some of which are for sale.

15W Gunnison Liquor House of Good Spirits, 603 West Tomichi Ave (West Highway 50) Gunnison, CO 81230   970 641-1717
N 38 o 32.633 W 106 o 56.010
Gunnison Liquor is a full-line liquor store with spirits, beers and wine. Watch for their weekly specials.

16W Love's Gas and Convenience Store, 655 West Tomichi Ave (West Highway 50) Gunnison, CO 81230 970 641-4045
N 38 o 32.661 W 106 o 56.076
Complete quick-stop convenience store with groceries, gasoline, ice and clean restrooms. Open early for coffee, breakfast sandwiches and more for early-morning anglers.

17W Scenic River Tours, 703 West Tomichi Ave. (West Highway 50) Gunnison, CO 81230   970 641-3131
N 38 o 32.662 W 106 o 56.097
Scenic River Tours offers a host of river running and rafting experiences on the Gunnison River throughout the summer.

Angling Guide to the

18W **Sportsman's Liquor,** 713 West Tomichi Ave. (West Highway
        50) Gunnison, CO 81230 970 641-3015
        N 38 o 32.681 W 106 o 56.119
A full service liquor store with spirits, wine and beer.

19W **Black Canyon Realty,** 600 W. Tomichi Ave. (West Highway
        50) Gunnison, CO 81230 970 641-4500
        N 38o 32.661 W 106o 56.005
Black Canyon Realty is located on the Tomichi Ave at the Blvd, and
specializes in acreage, home sites, and vacation homes and ranches.

20W **Pizza Hut,** 800 West Tomichi Ave (West Highway 50)
        Gunnison, CO 81230   970 641-3747
        N 38 o 32.675 W 106 o 56.187
Pizza Hut has both dine-in and take-out pizzas and free delivery.

21W **Star Texaco,** 821 West Tomichi Ave (West Highway 50)
        Gunnison, CO 81230 970 641-2912
        N 38 o 32.663 W 106 o 56.209
Star Texaco has gasoline, propane, ice and a convenience store.

22W **True Value Hardware,** 820 West Tomichi Ave. (West Highway
        50) Gunnison, CO 81230 (970-641-1212)
        N 38 o W 106 o
In addition to a line of hardware items, this store also carries a
complete line of camping, outdoor and fishing gear. Worms, bait, flies,
waders, crayfish tails, sucker meat, spinners and rod/reels are available.

23W **The Sundae Shop Restaurant,** 901 W. Tomichi Ave. (West
        Highway 50) Gunnison, CO 81230   970 641-5051
        N 38 o 32.640 W 106 o 56.246
The Sundae Shop is not an ice-cream parlor, but a great lunch and
dinner restaurant with reasonable prices, a comfortable casual
atmosphere and large portions. The specialties include everything from
chicken fried steak to a host of homemade hamburgers.

24W **A&W Restaurant,** 100 West New York Ave. Corner of New
        York and Highway 50 Gunnison, CO 81230   970 641-3089

N 38 o 32.593 W 106 o 56.347

Famous for Root Beer and floats, A&W has dine-in, patio, drive-in and take-out hamburgers, curly fries and BB-Q sandwiches.

25W Gunnison Ford/John Marzolf Automotive, 212 W. U.S. Highway 50 Gunnison, CO 81230 970 641-0051
   N 38o 32.464 W 106o 56.401

Gunnison's only authorized Ford/Mercury/Lincoln Mercury dealer and repair station.

26W Sun Sports Unlimited, 219 West Highway 50 Gunnison, CO 81230   (970-641-0883)
   N 38 o 32.420 W 106 o 56.385

Complete line of ATV's, motorcycles, boats, jet skis, snowmobiles and accessories for outdoor recreation

27W Hi-Country West Laundromat, 221 West Highway 50, Gunnison, CO 81230
   N38o 32.430 W 106o 56.372

Located at the west end of town, the Hi-Country West Laundromat is a great place to stop and clean sporting clothes after your angling and camping adventures. They are open from 7 am to 10 pm. Complete self-service laundry facilities including soap dispensers and change machines.

28W Public Dump Station, Gunnison, CO
   N 38o 32.126 W 106o 56.668

This public dump station and trash dump area is located off the service road behind the Day's Inn Motel. A self-service station, there's a $2 voluntary charge.

29W Cactus Jack's Restaurant and Lounge, 620 Rio Grande Ave. (Just off West Highway 50) Gunnison, CO 81230 970 641-2044
   N 38o 32.274 W 106o 56.307

Cactus Jack's atmosphere is casual and their Mexican food is excellent. In addition they specialize in great BB-Q, home style recipes. Open daily for lunch and dinner.

30W Gunnison County Airport, 711 Rio Grande Ave. Gunnison, Co 81230

N 38⁰ 32.293 W 106⁰ 56.195

Sporting one of the longest runways in the state of Colorado, the airport has numerous daily scheduled commercial flights that service many major airline hubs. In addition, 24-hour full private aircraft services are available. Rental cars, trucks, mini-vans and 4x4 vehicles are also available. Local transportation from the airport to Crested Butte is provided by Alpine Express 970 641-5074)

> Avis Rent A Car 970 641-0263
> Budget Rental Cars 970 641-4403
> Hertz Rent A Car 970 641-2881
> Gunnison Valley Aviation 970 641-0526

31W   Mergelman Lake, County Road 38 off of Highway 50
N 38⁰ 31.811 W 106⁰ 56.904

Located on the back side of the Gunnison County Airport, on County Road 38, Mergelman Lake is a small 2-acre pond that is stocked regularly by the DoW and provides a great place for close-to-town angling for stocked fish. Also, a great place to take the kids. It is located before the KOA campground.

32W Gunnison's KOA Campground, County Road 38, one-half mile off West U.S. Highway 50 Gunnison, CO 81230 970 641-1358
N 38⁰ 31.745 W 106⁰ 56.770

This KOA Family Campground has everything from large level grass sites, a stocked trophy trout pound, complete RV full hook ups, showers and restrooms, laundry facilities, gameroom, public phones, dump station and even cable TV and telephone hook ups. Day, week and seasonal rates are available.

33W Freddies Restaurant and Lounge, 1 1/2 miles west of Gunnison on West U.S. Highway 50 Gunnison, CO 81230 970 641-4748
N 38⁰ 31.756 W 106⁰ 57.531

Recently remodeled with a completely new menu, Freddies has a full service restaurant open for breakfast, lunch and dinner, as well as complete lounge. Music nightly, pool tables and live entertainment.

34W The Trough Restaurant and Lounge, 2 miles west of Gunnison
on West U.S. Highway 50 970 641-3724
N 38o 31.681 W 106o 57.745
This fine dinner house is well known for its steaks, wild game, seafood
and specialties. It also has a complete lounge with a host of live
entertainment.

Motels and Lodging

1M   **Blue Horizon Motel**, 2450 Highway 135 (3/4 mile North of Wal-Wart) at County Rd 11 Gunnison, CO 81230 970 641-6034
     N 38o 34.752 W 106o 55.336

A nice, small hotel with 10 Kitchenette units and Cable TV. Day, week and seasonal rates are available.

2M   **Days Inn**, 701 W. U.S. Highway 50 (Corner of West Highway 50 and Rio Grande) Gunnison, CO 81230 970 641-0608
     N 38o 32.258 W 106o 56.493

Clean and comfortable rooms at an affordable price with Jacuzzi, cable TV, laundry facilities and free continental breakfast.

3M   **Dos Rios Motor Hotel** , 1 1/2 miles west of Gunnison on West U.S. Highway 50 Gunnison, CO 81230 970 641-1000
     N 38o 31.775 W 106o 57.529

Recently completely remodeled, this small motor hotel has heated swimming pool and hot tub, cable TV and is located next to a great restaurant and lounge.

4M   **Gunnison's Hotel Row**, 500-300 block of E. Tomichi Ave (East Highway 50) Gunnison, CO 81230
     N 38o 32.654 W 106o 55.299

Within this two-block section are plenty of motels to suit just about every visitor's taste and budget. All are clean, neat and well-cared for. The staff members are friendly and the rates reasonable. Included in the line- up are the following:

5M   **ABC Motel**, 970 641-2400
     212 East Tomachi, Gunnison, CO 81230

6M   **Holiday Inn**, 970 641-1288
     400 East Tomachi, Gunnison, CO 81230

7M   **The Hylander Inn**, 970 641-0700
     412 East East Tomachi, Gunnison, CO 81230

8M **Mountain View Lodge,** 970 641-1799
117 North Taylor, Gunnison, CO 81230

9M **Super 8 Motel** 970 641-3068
411 East Tomachi, Gunnison, CO 81230

10M **Swiss Inn** 970 641-9962
312 East Tomachi, Gunnison

11M **Island Acres Motel,** 38339 W. U.S. Highway 50 Gunnison, CO
81230 970 641-1442
N 38o 32.004 W 106o 57.040
Literally located on an island in the Gunnison River, the Island Acres
Motel features affordable kitchenette rooms with cable TV.

12M **The Lazy K Resort/SilverSage Restaurant,** 1415 West
Tomichi Ave. Gunnison, CO 81230 970 641-5174 (800)
748-2295
N 38o 32.646 W 106o 56.697
Located at the edge of town in a very quiet setting, the Lazy K Resort
has summer cabins, condominiums and walk-in access to the Gunnison
River. In addition they have an on-site gourmet Western/Victorian
Restaurant and full-service bar that rates as one of the finest in the
Gunnison River Territory. Open daily for dinner and Sunday Brunch,
the SilverSage has a daily blackboard menu that specializes in Prime
Rib, Hand Cut Steaks and Chef's Selections.

13W **Long Holiday Motel,** 1198 W. Highway 50 Gunnison, CO
81230 970 641-0536
N 38o 32.066 W 106o 56.881
Located on the frontage road paralleling West Highway 50, the Long
Holiday Motel has 10 kitchenette units with cable TV. Daily, weekly
and seasonal rates are available.

14M **Mary Lawrence Inn,** 601 N Taylor Gunnison, CO 81230 970
641-3343
N 38o 33.016 W 106o 55.467
This exceptional Bed & Breakfast is in a fully-restored Victorian house.

The rooms and suites are luxurious, the breakfast is excellent and the hospitality unsurpassed. Advance reservations are strongly recommended!

15M **Park Inn Victorian Hotel,** 136 W. Tomichi Ave. (West Highway 50) Gunnison, CO 81230   970 641- 6834
   N 38 o 32.682 W 106 o 55.662

The Park Inn Victorian Hotel is located on Highway 50 and features rooms decorated and renovated in a true Victorian style. Antique furniture, claw-footed bathtubs and many hanging chandeliers abound for those that want to take a step back into history.

16M **Ramada Inn,** 1011 Rio Grande (Corner of Rio Grande and West Highway 50) Gunnison, CO 81230 970 641-2804
   N 38o 32.272 W 106o 56.455

A small Ramada Inn complete with indoor pool, spa, cable TV and free Continental breakfast.

17M **Tomichi Village Best Western Motel and Josef's Restaurant** 1-mile East on Highway 50 of Gunnison (East Highway 50) Gunnison, CO 81230 970 641-5032
   N 38o 32.699 W 106o 53.432

In addition to a fine Best Western Motel with plenty of rooms for visitors, Tomichi Village is also home to Josef's Restaurant which specializes in Alpine Cuisine.

18M **The Water Wheel Inn,** 2 miles West of Gunnison on West Highway 50 970 641-1650
   N 38o 31.657 W 106o 57.807

Modern hotel with cable TV, hot tub, exercise room and meeting facilities and free Continental breakfast.

19M **Wildwood Motel,** 1312 West Tomichi Ave. Gunnison, CO 81230 970 641-1663
   N 38o 32.669 W 106o 56.606

Off the beaten path of the main highway, The Wildwood Motel has 18 modern units complete with kitchens, cable TV and even spots with full RV hook-ups. They have weekly discounts for summer visitors.

Appendix A
Ancient And Early Blue Mesa History

To understand why the Gunnison River Territory (GRT) and the Blue
Mesa Reservoir are today top year-round outdoor recreation areas,
you have to go back some 37 million years ago, when violent volcanic
eruptions spewed fire-hot lava, rock and boiling mud over much of
what now is central and southwest Colorado. Indications of these
violent days are still graphically visible near the shores of Blue Mesa
Reservoir. The Dillon pinnacles, located above the north side of the
lake just past what is commonly called the Middle Bridge at Highway
50, are a maze of highly photographed vertical spires and towers cut
from the volcanic rock and mud that are known as a Breccia formation.

It may look rather desolate today, but in ancient times, it was
populated by a wide variety of dinosaurs. In recent years, dino-digging
scientists have uncovered a host of small to very large skeletons such
as the long necked dinosaurs Diplodocus, and Apatosaurus. Four intact
skeletons of Apatosaurus—formerly known as the Brontosaurus—have
recently been found, and U.C. Berkeley scientists are now trying to
figure out ways to protect them.

Nobody's really sure when man first arrived in what is now the
Gunnison Valley, and recent discoveries of nomadic Native American
tribe's wall structures could push back the "accepted dates" of human
population even further. What is definitely known is that early tribes
of native Americans often summered here.

Archaeologists have found evidence of habitation by these tribes
as long as 12,000 years ago. Historical data shows that these early
seasonal residents were big game hunters and plant gatherers. When
winter could be felt in the air, the tribes left the area and migrated to
warmer regions. After the spring thaw in the high country, they would
migrate back and often re-occupy their same camps.

In more modern times, it was the Ute Indians that occupied
today's region known as the Curecanti National Park, called so in
honor of the Ute Indian chief, Curicata. Short and muscular in terms
of physical build, the Utes were a peaceful and an isolated people who
co-existed with early white men settlers until late 1800's when miners
and settlers swarmed into the region. The Utes were divided into seven

tribal bands, with a total population of only about 10,000. Dark in color, and often referred to as black Indians by surrounding tribes, the group found here in the Gunnison area, were known as the Tabeguache or Uncompahgre Utes.

At the time of the Spanish explorers, the Ute Indian Nation claimed almost all of the entire state of what today is Colorado. They called themselves the Nuche, and by the mid 1600s, they were trading extensively with the Spanish for horses and other goods. By adopting the horse for their nomadic travels, the Nuche were better able to follow the migrating herds of buffalo over mountain passes and down into the plains. In fact today's modern Cochetopa Pass is Ute for "Pass of the Buffalo."

Over many thousands of years, the modern Gunnison River has been known by many names. To the Ute, it was Tomichi, meaning place of rocks and water. During the time of the Spaniards, it was called the Rio San Xavier. Later, the fur-trapping Mountain men called it the Grand River. Spanish came in search of gold, and mountain man came in search of fur. Such early explorers as Kit Carson, Bill Williams, Charles Autobees, Tom Tobin and even "Uncle" Dick Wooton trapped throughout the Gunnison area in 1830-1840's. However, fur trapping was sparse and difficult throughout Colorado's Rocky Mountains by comparison to Wyoming. According to the early trappers, Colorado's mountains were simply too high, there were too few rivers and as a consequence, not enough fur-bearing game.

By the mid-1850s, the push was on as to where and who would be the first to build a transcontinental railroad to effectively link east and the west. In March 1853, the U.S. Congress ordered four Pacific railroad surveys by Army engineers to find the "best route." Captain John Gunnison was charged with surveying the central railroad route between the 38th and 39th parallels for the Army's Topographical Engineers. With eleven years of wilderness surveying experience, he was given an escort of 32 mounted riflemen, 16 six-mule wagons, an instrument carriage, and an ambulance.

Upon first arriving in the region, Captain Gunnison found rich grassy meadows and a clear river of water. In his early writings about the area, it is clear he believed the region to be ideal for a railroad route. However, after further exploration, his opinion changed radically.

After a tough crossing of Cebolla Creek, his exploration party discovered that the going was only going to be rougher and tougher. After many miles of hiking, they discovered the nearly vertical 2,500 foot high walls of the Black Canyon, as well as its treacherous and turbulent white water. The canyon was shrouded in nearly perpetual twilight. Faced with continual natural obstacles, Gunnison and his party crossed the River at Lake Fork and decided to parallel the Black Canyon westward towards Montrose.

In the journals of that trip, Captain John Gunnison and his survey crew spent the entire 24 hours of September 9-10, 1853 crossing Rio de la Laguana. At some points, the wagons and mules had to be secured with ropes to keep from toppling over. Finally out of Lake Fork, Captain Gunnison headed southwest to avoid the Black Canyon entirely. However his party soon ran into troubles on the upper Blue Mesa where his men had to clear roads and literally carry wagons part of the way. The survey party continued overland to Cimarron and up and over the Cerro Summit (7,909 feet). They reached the Uncompahgre River on September 15th and followed it in a northwest direction past the present towns of Montrose, Olathe, and Delta. Paralleling the modern Gunnison river, the survey party trekked on to the present site of Grand Junction where the Gunnison and the Colorado Rivers come together today.

It was at this point that a wise Captain Gunnison wrote that the Black Canyon, the Blue Mesa, and the tough sage brush hills west of Lake Fork would make a railroad route through that area extremely impractical and prohibitively expensive.

Less than a month later and hundreds of miles to the west in Utah, John Gunnison and seven members of his survey party were attacked and killed by Paiute Indians. Ironically, the Paiute's attacked the Gunnison party out of revenge for the murder of one of their tribesmen, who had recently been killed by white settlers. Even though Gunnison's party had nothing to do with it, his men were killed and Gunnison's body was found riddled with 14 arrows.

Not until 1858 did the first major wagon train follow Captain Gunnison's route. However, the Gunnison River Territory quickly became known for its mountainous terrain too steep for a railroad route, and weather too severe for settlers.

The lull and tense peace between white explorers and the Utes was short lived, and there were numerous rumors that bullets made from gold were being used by the local Indians to drive off settlers. By 1859 the Colorado Gold Rush was on in earnest. In 1861 and 1862, Washington Gulch, north of Crested Butte had a mining camp with a population of over 200. In those two years, they mined over a million dollars in gold through placer mining.

In the summer of 1862, the Utes, angered by the white man's invasion of their hunting grounds, attacked and killed 12 miners in Washington Gulch. The gold strike there was playing out, and only a few hardy miners remained after the attack, living on game and fish from the local mountains. Constantly harassed by Indians, those miners who stayed found they needed rifle and shovel, hand-in-hand.

With the numerous government surveys, discovery of gold at Pikes Peak, and the continual influx of white settlers, pressure mounted to have the Ute Indians removed from the area. According to historical references, the Ute Indian's complete lack of tribal organization was good for miners that came into the Gunnison and San Juan counties. Realizing the difficulty in trying to deal with a host of individual Indian bands, the U.S. Government insisted that all talks and negotiations take place through one Supreme Chief. In 1868, a 35 year old Tabeguache Ute, Chief Ouray, became the spokesman for the seven tribes.

These were turbulent times in the Gunnison River territory. Miners were constantly trespassing on Ute lands, and the Indian's reservation kept shrinking. After the Utes refused to sell the mineral rights to the San Juan's, Chiefs Ouray and Curicata went to Washington DC to meet President Ulysses S. Grant in order to see "first hand," the white man's power and his cities. It worked. By 1873, Utes had ceded nearly 4,000,000 acres of land to United States. As part of the agreement, the Utes were allowed to continue to hunt on their former lands as long as there were no conflicts with white miners or settlers. In return for cessation of these lands, the Utes would receive $25,000 per year, with Chief Ouray receiving an additional $1,000 per year, as long as he remained the Ute chief.

By this treaty, the Utes were placed on a reservation located in the western third of Colorado—the future sites of modern-day Gunnison and Crested Butte were outside the reservation boundaries.

In 1875, the Utes were moved to the Uncompahgre reservation, 12 miles south of present day Montrose.

In 1880 and 1881, the Utes were again moved, this time to a small reservation in Utah. Today, however, the Utes have returned to their ancestral lands in the Gunnison basin. They have made extensive purchases of the plateau land around the Blue Mesa Reservoir that borders the Curecanti Recreation Area.

Colorado entered the Union as the 30th state in August 1876. In 1877, the State legislature formed Gunnison County which encompassed some 10,600 square miles. During the late 1800s, after the Ute Indians were completely displaced, thousands of miners swarmed into the area and created the towns of Telluride, Lake City, Ouray, Silverton, and numerous others. As what today is commonly called the Western Slope, continued to develop, Gunnison County was reduced in size to some 3,000 square miles.

With all of the local Indians being removed, and many of the gold-rich areas snapped up in the San Juans, gold hungry prospectors spilled into the Gunnison River territory in 1879 and gold was discovered in Taylor Park and on Tomichi Creek. The town of Crested Butte sprang into being because it was at head of the Elk Mountains and Gunnison, strategically located at a juncture of the Gunnison River and Tomichi Creek, flourished.

As can be imagined, in the late 1800s, roads were primitive and sometimes nonexistent. Stage coach lines proved unprofitable because of the distances involved, and soon, the railroad was on it's way. William Jackson Palmer was a Civil War veteran and ambitious entrepreneur. He secured a million dollar bond issue and financed the construction of the first narrow gauge railroad system in Colorado. Called the Denver and Rio Grande Railway, its rails were only three feet apart—compared to the standard gauge of 4-feet 8-inches. The narrow gauge tracks required far less labor to construct, used lighter rolling stock and required smaller bridges in the mountainous terrain.

General Palmer envisioned a north-to-south railroad route that would run from Denver to El Paso, Texas. It would then connect with railroads that ran into Mexico. Once out of Denver, the route went through Colorado Springs, through Pueblo and Canon City, and then over Marshall Pass and into Gunnison. Trains regularly dropped passengers at hunting and fishing lodges at Iola, Cebolla and Sapinero—areas now under the waters of the modern Blue Mesa Reservoir.

However, the route down into the Black Canyon was so formidable, that the narrow gauge railroad could only leave the canyon at the town of Cimarron, where the rails switched to the standard gauge system. From 1882 to 1936, the railway system known as the "DE and RG" "Scenic Line of the World" transported gold and silver ore, coal, cattle and passengers. The last train through the Black Canyon made its journey in 1949. When it reached Cimarron, an epic age in the history of the Gunnison River Territory came to an end.

Appendix B
The Birth of the Blue Mesa Reservoir

Since the late 1800s, the Gunnison River Territory (GRT) has been dependent on the visiting outdoor recreationalist. Even the first narrow-gauge railroad system dropped visitors off along the right-of-way to hunt and fish at locations such as Iola, Cebolla and Sapinero. While all these stops are now under water, they remain popular angling and boating "map locations" on the modern Blue Mesa Reservoir.

Phil Zickerman is Chief of Interpretation, U.S. National Park Service at the Gunnison River Territory's Curecanti Recreation Area on the Blue Mesa Reservoir. Holding this position for the last seven years, he rates as one of the experts on the Blue Mesa on all facets of the history and use of this, the largest lake in Colorado.

Phil points out that as with many regions in the Western United States, water is life. The proper and careful use water for everything from ranching and irrigation to recreation is paramount in terms of human habitation and proper recreational use.

One hundred years ago, the Gunnison was a free-flowing river that sported a population of native Colorado River cutthroats. Proper management techniques were even then being practiced. Brook trout were introduced in 1883, rainbow trout in 1888 and German Brown trout in 1893. But as the 19th Century came to a close, all that began to change with the construction of a massive water-diverting tunnel down in the modern Montrose area that even today is listed in as a National Civil Engineering Landmark.

In the later part of the 1950s, Colorado Congressman, Wayne Aspinal took the initiative as a result of legislation in 1956 that called for the construction of large water storage areas that could be used for agriculture, and the generation of electric power. The waters of the free-flowing Gunnison River were prime candidates, and three dams were proposed. The legislation created the Blue Mesa Reservoir dam for water storage, the Morrow Point Reservoir dam for hydro-electric production, and the Crystal Reservoir dam for water regulation.

Under the direction of the U.S. Government's Bureau of Reclamation, the time line on the three newly created reservoirs was as follows: 1) Blue Mesa Reservoir, completed in 1965, 2) Morrow Point Reservoir, completed in 1968, 3) Crystal Reservoir, completed in 1977. Citizens of the area have teamed with state and federal officials to assure that the water resources represented in this massive reservoir complex will be managed properly.

Appendix C
Where To Find Information about . . .

Colorado Division of Wildlife
6060 Broadway
Denver, CO 80216 - Phone: (303) 297-1192

U.S. Forest Service
P.O. Box 25127
Lakewood, CO 80225 - Phone: (303) 236-9431

Colorado Division of Parks and Outdoor Recreation
1313 Sherman St.
Denver, CO 80203 - Phone: (303) 866-3437

U.S. Bureau of Land Management
2850 Youngfield
Lakewood, CO 80215 - Phone: (303) 236-21 00

U.S. Geological Survey
P.O. Box 25286,
Denver Federal Center
Denver, CO 80225 - Phone: (303) 236-7477

Colorado Campground Association
5101 Pennsylvania Ave.
Boulder, CO 80970 - Phone: (303) 499-9343

Colorado Highway Department
4201 E. Arkansas Ave.
Denver, CO 80222 - Phone: (303) 757-9011

Colorado State Museum and Historical Society
1300 Broadway
Denver, CO 80203 - Phone: (303) 866-3682

About the Author

Andy Lightbody has been a life-long outdoorsperson. Fishing, hunting, camping and writing about it all of his life, he has been the Managing Editor for *Western Outdoors Magazine*, Senior Editor for Petersen's *Hunting Magazine* and Editor of the Outdoor Book Division for *Guns & Ammo*. Currently, he is the Regional Editor for *Fishing & Hunting News*, a correspondent for *Fish & Game Finder Magazine*, host of the syndicated radio program, "Outdoor Minutes," Outdoor Columnist to many local and regional newspapers, and a regular contributor to many of the national and international sporting publications and journals.

His writings, photos and consulting contributions/assistance have appeared in *Outdoor Life*, *In-Fisherman*, *North American Fishing Club*, Trout Unlimited's *Streamside*, *Rocky Mountain Game & Fish*, *Fly Fisherman*, The *Rocky Mountain News*, Business Radio Network, ESPN Television, NHK Television" (Japan) and Radio New Zealand.

Andy lives with his wife, Tari, and four children in Gunnison, Colorado where he now spends his time teaching his three sons and one daughter about the outdoors, conducting his syndicated radio shows and happily writing about fishing and hunting in the Gunnison River Territory.

Blue Mesa Reservoir

Index

Blue Mesa Reservoir

114

Gunnison Sporting Goods

Your One-stop Fishing Headquarters

Locally owned and operated, with plenty of expert advice on where the fish are always biting. We stock everything from rods and reels to licenses, topo maps to fishing tackle. And we specialize in bait, flies—and hunting supplies, as well.

Show us this ad and with the purchase of 6 fishing flies, we'll give you the 7th, free!

133 E. Tomichi Gunnison, CO 81230 970 641-5022

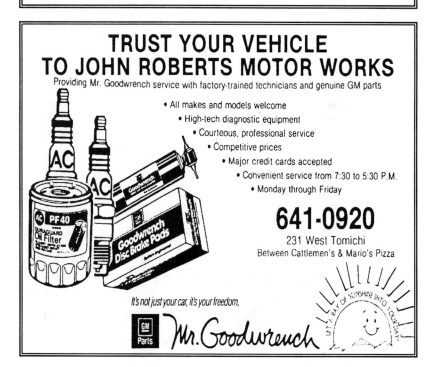

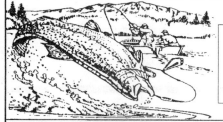
117

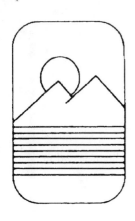

Blue Mesa Ranch
Gunnison, Colorado

We invite you to join us for '5 Star' Resort Camping

With this ad you can enjoy

3 DAYS & 2 NIGHTS *Free Camping . . .*

In addition

there will be a very SPECIAL GIFT *waiting for you!*

Blue Mesa Ranch is located on Colorado's largest lake, the Blue Mesa Reservoir. Enjoy great boating, fishing, hiking . . . plus all the amenities the resort has to offer . . . Indoor Pool, hot tub, miniature golf, horseback riding, full time activities and much, much more.

Call now for reservations at **(970) 641-0492**, and bring this ad with you when you visit.

27601 West Highway 50 — Gunnison, Colorado 81230